Collin

LITTLE BOO

C000244073

IRISH
HISTORY

Neil Hegarty

HarperCollins Publishers
Westerhill Road
Bishopbriggs
Glasgow
G64 2QT

First Edition 2020

Reprint 10 9 8 7 6 5 4 3 2 1

© HarperCollins Publishers 2020

ISBN 978-0-00-834013-1

Collins® is a registered trademark
of HarperCollins Publishers
Limited

www.collins.co.uk

A catalogue record for this book is
available from the British Library

Author: Neil Hegarty

Typeset by Davidson Publishing
Solutions

Printed and bound in China by
RR Donnelley APS Co Ltd

HarperCollins does not warrant
that www.collins.co.uk or any other
website mentioned in this title will
be provided uninterrupted, that
any website will be error free, that
defects will be corrected, or that the
website or the server that makes
it available are free of viruses or
bugs. For full terms and conditions
please refer to the site terms
provided on the website.

Contents

Introduction

From the very beginnings of its history, the island of Ireland has been open to the influence of the surrounding world. The seas that separate Ireland from its European neighbours might seem, on the face of it, to act as barriers, dividing the inhabitants of Ireland from international affairs. In fact, the opposite has always been the case, for the seas have acted as highways, bringing foreign influences, goods and traffic, travellers, wanderers, and invaders to Irish shores.

This, then, is an island with a history woven into a much larger tapestry – and the pages of this book demonstrate this international dimension in Irish history time and again. The first inhabitants of Ireland arrived from abroad, as the ice sheets retreated and the seas rose, and they have continued to arrive from overseas. The work of acculturation – of newcomers putting down roots in a new land, trading, farming, connecting in human, cultural, social, and economic ways – can be seen consistently at play, and this process complicates the narratives of invasion and conquest that form such dominant themes in Irish history.

Of course, armed invasions have indeed recurred throughout Irish history and they were ferocious in nature.

In their wake came death, starvation, and dispossession, with the poor, the old, women, and children bearing the brunt of the violence, and no history worth the name can sidestep such brutal facts. This book traces the nature and character of such episodes, some of which are better known than others. The incursion of Scottish armies into Ireland brought ruin to the land, but this fourteenth-century episode is less well remembered than the Cromwellian invasion of the seventeenth century, which devastated Irish society, causing the deaths of hundreds of thousands of Irish men, women, and children. The figure of Oliver Cromwell himself is remembered in England as a proto-democrat, but in Ireland his name is associated with gruesome violence and genocide. Such episodes are worth dwelling on, for they remind us that if a history is to be truly meaningful, it must illuminate the experience of the defeated, as well as that of the victor.

Stubborn political dogma and wilful blindness have also played malignant roles in the story of Ireland, and this is nowhere better exemplified than in the events of the Great Famine of the nineteenth century. This is Ireland's defining social, economic, emotional, and demographic fracture. It offers a dreadful reminder that violence and trauma in history take many forms, and leave a mark upon society for generations to come.

This book attends to the complexity of Ireland past and present: to its writers and its architecture, its landscape and natural world, its religions, artefacts, and sports, and to the imprint and lasting influence of the ancient Irish language. It traces the stories of its politics and its divisions. One such division – the political border that runs through the island today – has seldom been out of the headlines in recent years. The violence it has engendered and the political tensions that surround it are examined too in all their fraught complexity, together with the facts surrounding the creation of two Irish states in the modern era, and the trajectories of their society and politics. The nature of the peace process in Northern Ireland, the progressive politics that have emerged in a Republic of Ireland that was once a bastion of Catholicism in Europe: these issues and more are explored – all with an eye on a future that, in an age of Brexit, is remarkably, startlingly plastic.

Ireland is, in demographic terms, a young country, with an eye on the future: it has embraced modernity and is open to European and global influences. And yet, it remains a singular place, and mindful of the past. This Little Book illuminates many elements in this past and, in the process, it offers a reminder that, in understanding our history, we can also better understand our present world.

About the author

Neil Hegarty grew up in Derry. His non-fiction books include *The Secret History of Our Streets* (2012), which tells the story of twentieth-century London; *The Story of Ireland* (2011), which accompanies the BBC-RTE television history of Ireland; and *Frost: That Was the Life That Was* (2015), the biography of television interviewer David Frost. Neil's novels include *Inch Levels* (2016) and *The Jewel* (2019). He lives in Dublin.

Mesolithic Ireland

The human story of Ireland begins around 13,000 years ago, with the retreat of the glaciers that had covered the country during the Ice Age, followed by a slow rise in sea levels. Meadows and then scant woods of juniper and birch spread across the land, followed as the centuries passed by dense broadleaf forests. The land that became Ireland was possibly not yet an island, for land-bridges may have offered paths from Britain. However, it is clear that by 7000 BC human hunter-gatherers had crossed by land or sea to establish a permanent presence in Ireland, felling trees, spreading along the river valleys, and hewing out a livelihood amid populations of wolves, bears, boar, and smaller mammals. They dwelt in skin-roofed huts. Excavations of early settlements – on the banks of the river Bann at Mountsandel in County Derry, for example – reveal eloquent remains in the form of charcoal left by fires, flint worked into axe-heads, animal bones, and the ubiquitous shells of hazelnuts that were a mainstay of the Mesolithic diet. The population waxed and waned as the climate warmed and cooled: by 4000 BC, it is estimated that there were fewer than 10,000 people living in Ireland.

The Céide Fields

On the windswept sea cliffs of north County Mayo lie the Céide Fields: a hypnotizing jigsaw of tiny fields that date from the Neolithic period, which began c. 3500 BC. Exploration of the area commenced in the 1930s, when areas of the blanket bog covering the landscape was excavated, to reveal a tracery of stone walls – clearly the work of ancient hands. These fields and walls offered the first hard evidence for the existence of early farming in Ireland: indeed, the Céide Fields represent the oldest extant field systems to be found anywhere in the world. They demonstrate that the sparse population of hunter-gatherers that spread across Ireland during the Mesolithic period had now become agriculturalists. Possibly they crossed using a still surviving land-bridge between Britain and Ireland, or by sea in light skin boats, bringing with them domesticated flocks of sheep, goats, and cows. The dense ancient forests vanished, replaced by pasture, and by arable fields in which were sown primitive strains of barley and wheat. Larger and more established settlements developed, with more elaborate dwellings of wood, wattle and daub, and thatch.

Newgrange

In the fertile lowlands of County Meath rises the spectacular Neolithic site at Newgrange. This great monument was established c. 3200 BC, making it considerably more venerable than Stonehenge or the Pyramids, and it takes the form of a vast domed mound enclosing passages and inner chambers, with walls adorned by a range of carvings. Evidently, the structure was designed according to strict astronomical calculations: today, on the winter solstice, the first rays of the rising sun enter the mound and flood the innermost chamber with light. Newgrange is one element in Brú na Bóinne, a complex of Neolithic sites ranged along the Boyne river valley. These sites in turn are just some among many Neolithic monuments – such as the Poulnabrone dolmen in County Clare and Carrowmore in County Sligo – that still survive in Ireland. Each such site shares many similarities with other Neolithic monuments scattered across Europe, suggesting close connections between a range of dispersed civilizations. Newgrange is bound up with Irish myth but its essential function is still unknown. As such, it exemplified the ability of ancient humans in Ireland to leave lasting, remarkable, but essentially mysterious imprints on the landscape.

History and Myth: Cúchulainn

The great hero and warrior Cúchulainn is a central figure of ancient Irish mythology, and is particularly connected with the northern province of Ulster. In one of many versions of the story, he was conceived at Newgrange as the son and incarnation of the powerful god Lug and of Deichtine, daughter of the king of Ulster. Stories of Cúchulainn's talents in love and war are legion: one such tale, that of the Cattle Raid of Cooley, sees the hero pitted against Medb (Maeve), the strong-willed and ambitious Queen of the western province of Connacht, whose armies invade Ulster to seize its prize stud bull. Cúchulainn wins the day by defeating one enemy warrior after another in single combat, in a display of might that lasts for many months. By turns capable of ferocious anger and of great gentleness and sensitivity, Cúchulainn has been invoked in support of a range of groups over the years. To Irish nationalists, for example, he stands for heroic independence, power, stamina, and ferocity in the face of adversity; equally, he has been claimed by unionists as a symbolic bulwark against invasion from the south.

The Celts

Ireland is famously a 'Celtic' nation, sharing strong cultural and linguistic traits with other 'Celtic' societies in Scotland, Wales, Cornwall, Brittany, and the Isle of Man – but what does 'Celtic' actually mean? The term is a vexed one: it first entered common use during a period of rising nationalism in nineteenth-century Ireland and became a useful means to distinguish Irish culture from that of 'Anglo-Saxon' England. As for the facts, it was long claimed that Ireland was occupied by waves of Celtic invaders arriving from central Europe around 500 BC, who supplanted the existing culture that had developed in the course of the preceding centuries. In addition, legend speaks of a period in deepest antiquity, when the 'Milesians' sailed to Ireland from Iberia to do battle with the Tuatha dé Danaan, the existing inhabitants of the land. But recent research reveals no such invasion: instead, newcomers arrived steadily from across the sea, acclimatizing and adapting to life in an already populated land, and adding their experience to the cultural mix – but, crucially, not erasing the civilization that had gone before. 'Celtic', then, is a useful mark of cultural identity, rather than a concept rooted firmly in historical fact.

Dún Aonghasa

The great fortress of Dún Aonghasa lies on the sheer cliffs along the south coast of Inis Mór (Inishmore), the largest of the Aran Islands. It was memorably described by the Victorian archaeologist George Petrie as the 'most magnificent barbaric monument extant in Europe': it is indeed truly spectacular, and its setting against a panorama of ocean and sky adds to the drama. Dún Aonghasa takes the form of a series of concentric stone walls which end on the cliff edge: it is assumed these walls originally enclosed a circular space, but the remainder of the site has collapsed over the centuries into the Atlantic. The fortress was built and rebuilt over the aeons, but it is thought that the first stronghold on this site dates from approximately 1100 BC. Although much of its history is lost, one can surmise that the site grew in size and complexity over the years. For example, the so-called *cheval de frise* – the dense fields of jagged rocks placed deliberately around the site – demonstrates the importance of Dún Aonghasa as a place of defence, and speaks eloquently of an otherwise shadowed prehistory of war, attack, and defence scored onto the landscape of modern Ireland.

The Broighter Hoard

Ancient Ireland was a place of conflict and struggle, but it was also characterized by intense artistry and creativity. The National Gallery of Ireland's collection provides evidence of this creativity in the form of an immense treasury of Irish gold: jewellery, sheet gold, lunulae and torcs (golden collars or rings), bracelets and earrings – much of it highly and cleverly decorated. Gold was panned from the rivers of Ireland, particularly those flowing from the uplands where seams were known to exist, such as the Wicklow Mountains in Leinster and the Sperrin Mountains in Ulster. Much of this worked gold was buried, plundered, or dispersed over the years – and uncovered by accident. One startling find was the Broighter Hoard, revealed in 1896 by a farmer ploughing his fields on the edge of Lough Foyle in County Derry. He discovered a wooden box filled with gold from the first century BC, including the Broighter Torc and other ornaments, plus the Broighter Boat, fragile but intact and fashioned exquisitely. The hoard is speculated to have been a votive offering to the sea god Manannán Mac Lir, and sunk into what had been the ancient sea-bed.

Hibernia and Rome

By the third century BC, classical maps featured Ierne, an island on the edge of the world, and by the beginning of the first millennium, Ierne was the Roman *Hibernia*: land of winter. Yet Ireland was not on the margins of knowledge – on the contrary: trading routes encompassed the shores of the Atlantic islands, and Ireland exported animal skins, cattle, butter, and wolfhounds. The Romans, then, had a good working knowledge of Ireland, but there was no great incentive to conquer the island. Hibernia was – more or less – manageable from afar, despite the occasional raids by Irish pirates and slavers on the western coasts of the new Roman province of Britannia. History glimpses only one moment when the Romans contemplated an invasion of Ireland: in AD 82, Tacitus speaks of an Irish prince who travelled to Britannia to enlist the military assistance of the Roman general Agricola in resolving a dispute at home. Agricola maintained a fleet in south-west Scotland, from where the coasts of Hibernia were clearly visible – but his attention was diverted by a Scottish uprising. Roman legions would never cross the sea to Ireland.

Before Christianity

The prince who had enlisted the assistance of Agricola was one of many such leaders, for Ireland at this time was divided into a series of kingdoms or *túatha*, the borders of which fluctuated ceaselessly. The *túatha* did from time to time federate into larger entities, but these too were subject to continual change. Even the five historic provinces of Ulster, Munster, Leinster, Connacht, and Meath were by no means constant fixtures on the political scene. There was certainly no conception of a centralized state, and yet there was the sense of a collective identity. Significantly, the Irish word for a province was *cúige*, meaning a fifth, thus implying the presence or existence of a whole. In social and economic terms, these were intensely hierarchical societies: power flowed from the king through the scribes and poets – whose influence in an oral culture was considerable – down to the landless serfs. Laws were pervasive and byzantine, governing every aspect of life, and so, in spite of political turmoil and competition, life in Ireland was inherently deeply stable and organized. This was a society in which each individual knew their place.

Palladius: the 'first Patrick'

By the second half of the fourth century AD, a small but established Christian community was in existence in Ireland. It was focused in the south-eastern corner of the country: that part of the island most in contact with the ebb and flow of power and culture in the Roman world, and with the doctrinal disputes that regularly convulsed early Christendom. Indeed, it was to ensure the doctrinal purity of Ireland's Christian community that Celestine I, Pope from 422–432, dispatched the first envoy to Ireland. As the historian Prosper of Aquitaine put it: 'To the Irish believing in Christ, Palladius, having been ordained by Pope Celestine, is sent as first bishop.' Palladius landed with a small group of companions on the coast of what is now County Wicklow around AD 428, and ministered largely in this part of the country. But Palladius' sojourn was brief: he was unable to navigate the mazes of Irish political life, fell out of favour with local Irish kings – and within three years had departed Ireland for Scotland. Though remembered in local folk culture, Palladius and his legacy have been almost entirely erased from official Irish histories.

Patrick: myth and reality

Few historical figures loom larger in Irish history than Patrick: patron saint, evangelist, and politician. He grew up in late Roman Britain, early in the fifth century AD. The standard stories speak of his capture by Irish slavers, who brought him to Ireland. Here he was put to work as a goatherd for some years before eventually making his way home to Britain; later, the adult Patrick returned to an ostensibly pagan Ireland to spread the Good News, and convert the Irish to Christianity. As we know, some of this story is untrue, for Christianity had established itself well before Patrick's arrival, but his ministry was influential. He was a vigorous and skilled communicator, for example deploying the existing Irish practice of worshipping gods in groups of three in order to explain the Christian doctrine of the Trinity. He had, moreover, political skills absent in Palladius: he was able to enlist the powerful Irish kings to his cause, thus rapidly building a following across the land. By the time of his death late in the fifth century, Christianity had imprinted itself indelibly across the land.

Pilgrimage

The silvery peak of Croagh Patrick rises to 764 metres, and overlooks the island-flecked expanse of Clew Bay in west County Mayo. The mountain is nicknamed the 'Reek', and it has long been a significant place of pilgrimage in Ireland. On Reek Sunday – the last Sunday in July each year – thousands of walkers (some of them barefoot) climb the mountain and attend a Christian service in the small chapel on its summit. The Reek itself owes its importance to Patrick – the saint is said to have spent forty days fasting on the mountain in AD 441 – and the summer pilgrimage has survived for centuries. Nor is Croagh Patrick the only significant place of Patrician pilgrimage in Ireland today. County Donegal is home to St Patrick's Purgatory on Station Island in Lough Derg, which similarly has been a sacred site for hundreds of years. Patrick's remains are said to lie in Down Cathedral in County Down; and a statue of the saint stands on the Hill of Slane in County Meath, where Patrick is said to have lit the Easter Flame, or Paschal Flame, thus ushering in the age of Irish Christianity.

'Saints and Scholars'

The collapse of the Roman Empire in western Europe
may not have led to the 'Dark Ages' of myth, but it
did contribute to a steep decline in cultural activity
and written records. In Ireland, conversely, these years
saw a startling flowering in creativity – the result of
the spread of Christianity and the establishment of
great monasteries across the land. As the existing
oral culture gave way to the written word, so copious
records began to be kept detailing every aspect of life.
In scriptoria up and down Ireland, monks created the
famous 'illuminated' manuscripts, which stand today
as exemplars of Ireland's status as a place of 'saints and
scholars'. The monasteries fulfilled many significant
functions: they maintained social stability; provided
housing, health services, and places of incarceration;
acted as places of education; and, not least, fuelled
economic growth, as they directed and channelled
the agricultural output of their district. Such great
monasteries as Clonmacnoise, on the river Shannon in
County Offaly, were famous across Europe, and from its
quays, goods flowed across Ireland. The abbots of such
institutions became key players and arbiters of power
and authority on the local political scene.

Glendalough

The highland valley of Glendalough in County Wicklow, with its twin lakes and its glorious backdrop of granite hills, is today one of Ireland's most prominent tourist attractions. It has been significant in Irish history since the sixth century, when St Kevin established a place of hermitage here, and settled into a life of contemplation and prayer. Kevin's reputation for piety and austerity drew pilgrims to the valley, where a monastery and seminary were established. Following Kevin's death c. 618, the settlement flourished for centuries. The site today contains significant monastic remnants, which testify to the size and scale of Glendalough at its height: most famous is the great round tower, which dominates the valley. Kevin is a man for all ages, and today his life is interpreted as one of environmental awareness. Seamus Heaney's famous poem 'St Kevin and the Blackbird' responds to the folk legend that describes the saint sitting in contemplation, arms outstretched, when a blackbird settles in the palm of his hand, nests, and lays her eggs. Rather than disturb the bird, Kevin remains in his position 'until the young are hatched and fledged and flown'.

Dál Riata

The seas surrounding Ireland were far from being a barrier to trade, communication, and human interaction. Quite the opposite was the case: they enabled a flow of goods and people over the centuries – and this fact is made manifest in the form of Dál Riata, a kingdom that spanned the channel between western Scotland and the Irish province of Ulster. The origins of Dál Riata lie in the early centuries of the first millennium, although the precise facts remain unproven. For many years historians posited the idea of an Irish conquest of south-west Scotland. Today, however, theories favour the idea of an essentially organic evolution of the kingdom, as the natural result of a kinship between two closely related territories. This latter theory underscores the sense of relative ease of human communication and travel across the seas. Dál Riata was an important centre for maritime trade. It endured as a kingdom until the eighth century, when military and political changes in both Ireland and Scotland led to its gradual eclipse and disappearance from the records, and the rise of the kingdom of Scotland in its place.

Colm Cille

The centuries-long closeness between Ireland and Scotland is best encapsulated in the history of St Colm Cille. He was born at Gartan in County Donegal in 521, and his life captures the mingling of civil authority, ecclesiastical law, and politics that shaped the society of the time. Colm Cille founded the great monasteries at Derry and Durrow, before leaving Ireland to establish the monastery on Iona, at the heart of Dál Riata territory, and he was a key player in the politics of that kingdom. Having established his power base on Iona, the saint took to intervening in the governance of Dál Riata. Such was his influence that a summit was convened in 575 between the leaders of Dál Riata and the Uí Néill, who governed much of the north of Ireland. The result of the summit was an agreement that Dál Riata would formally bind itself to the Uí Néill, thus establishing a kingdom spanning the seas. As for the cultural legacy of Colm Cille's Iona, this was immense. The exquisite Book of Kells was begun here; and it was from the island that other missionaries went forth to establish monasteries at Lindisfarne, and further afield.

Columbanus in Europe

As the culture and politics of Ireland influenced Britain, so they influenced Europe too. In these years, many Irish *peregrinari*, or wandering monks, travelled the continent, imprinting specifically Irish influences on European life, and the first and most famous of these was St Columbanus (540–615). Columbanus comes down to us as a distinctly forbidding individual, for he was given to a life of fearsome austerity – including starvation rations and limited sleep – the better to conquer the intrinsic sinfulness of his human nature. Born in the province of Leinster, he studied in the monastery at Bangor in County Down, before departing for exile in France. Here he founded three monasteries, complete with tonsured monks and a stricter-than-strict code governing every conceivable aspect of life. However, his dauntless attitude to life and scorn for authority – he even picked a fight with the Pope of the day – led at length to his banishment from France, and years of further wandering. His last and greatest monastery was at Bobbio, in what is now northern Italy, but at least sixty such institutions were founded in his name, and generations of his monks fanned out across Europe, disseminating Latin literature and knowledge in the process.

The Irish language

Irish – *Gaeilge* – is an ancient tongue, one of the oldest
languages in Europe. Its beginnings are shadowy but,
by the beginning of the first millennium, it was spoken
across Ireland, with closely related tongues used in
Scotland and the Isle of Man. Evidence of the first written
Irish script comes in the form of Ogham: fourth- and
fifth-century stone carvings still to be found today across
Ireland; later, scholars adopted the Latin alphabet for
written Irish. Ireland today is officially a bilingual state.
Under the Irish Constitution, *Gaeilge* holds the status
of 'first official language'; it is also an official language
of the EU. In visual terms, it is ubiquitous: to be seen
on every road sign, and on all state documents; and
study of the language is compulsory throughout the
school system in the Republic of Ireland. In practice,
the language has dwindled over the centuries: today, its
everyday use is largely limited to *Gaeltacht* areas along
the Atlantic seaboard. However, in Northern Ireland and
in urban areas in the Republic, where *Gaelscoileanna*,
or Irish-language schools, are increasingly popular, the
language is witnessing something of a revival.

Skellig Michael

The most extraordinary – and remote, and elemental – of
Irish monasteries was the settlement on Skellig Michael
(Sceilg Mhichíl), a crag of rock that lies in the
Atlantic some seven miles west of County Kerry's Iveragh
peninsula. The twin-peaked silhouette of the Skellig, as
viewed from the mainland, is one of the most evocative
of Irish sights. The island is a World Heritage Site and
an important and abundant bird sanctuary; and it has
recently gained new global fame as the hidden hermitage
of Luke Skywalker in the latest *Star Wars* films. The Skellig
has a venerable history, for at some point between the
sixth and eighth centuries AD, monks crossed from
the mainland to found a settlement in this extreme
environment. The monastery was established on a
terraced slope 180 metres above the sea and a hermitage
was built below the island's south peak. The settlement
endured until the twelfth or thirteenth century and
remained a place of regular pilgrimage in the following
centuries. Today, visiting is possible in the summer
months: flights of stone steps lead from a landing
place to the monastic remains, with their characteristic
'beehive' cells and tremendous ocean views.

Illumination

The so-called 'illuminated' manuscripts are the greatest cultural glories to have emerged from Ireland's early Christian era. These were books, on vellum, richly decorated with elaborate borders and illustration. Many cultures through the ages have created such 'illuminated' books: the Irish variety included reproductions of Gospel and other Biblical stories, and the best known of them today is the Book of Kells. This manuscript was written in Latin, and it brings together all four Gospels, plus an assortment of other texts, into one vast book. It is ornately decorated with swirling motifs and images of humans, birds, and beasts, and is richly and lavishly coloured. The Book of Kells was created around AD 800, probably on Iona. It is likely to have been completed in the abbey at Kells in County Meath, and it remained in Kells until 1654, when it was sent to Dublin, where it has been held in the Library of Trinity College since 1661. But the monks of Ireland did not limit themselves to sacred texts: everything from classical myth to the *Táin* – the great Irish myth cycle of Cúchulainn and Queen Medb – was similarly included in a new and burgeoning literary culture.

'Heathen men'

The end of monastic Ireland's glory days can be dated precisely to AD 795, when the monastery on the island of Rathlin was sacked by ferocious raiders who came over the sea. These were the Vikings – the Norsemen – and the first sighting of them in British waters had been two years previously, when their ships had appeared off the shores of the famous Northumbrian monastery at Holy Island, or Lindisfarne. Now these Vikings – as the *Anglo-Saxon Chronicle* gloomily put it, these 'heathen men' who came with 'rapine and slaughter' – were in Ireland, and their impact would be immediate, profound, and long-lasting. In the years after the Rathlin attack, coastal and island monasteries were attacked again and again, and their treasuries plundered. Iona came under assault in 802 and 806, and gradually many monasteries were abandoned, with communities moving inland to find safety. Such security, however, was not easily achieved: the light, shallow-draughted Viking ships could sail as easily on the rivers of Ireland as they could along its coasts. Soon Vikings were scouting the river Shannon and establishing bases on inland lakes. The great inland monastery at Clonmacnoise was torched in 835.

The Viking presence

These Vikings are popularly remembered as bloodthirsty marauders, invariably out to loot and pillage, but it is important to remember that the history of these years was written by the monks, who were not disposed to look kindly on the Norse and their activities in Ireland. And indeed, the truth is that there is a great deal more to the history of the Vikings in Ireland than bloodshed and violence. They traded as much as they raided – raided for Church booty (altar treasures and jewelled bibles); traded in jet, glass, and leather, and in slaves – and, as is the way with invaders, they gradually settled in Ireland, intermarried, and became players on the domestic economic and political scene. They established settlements at Limerick, Cork, Youghal, Wexford, Arklow, and Waterford, and these grew rapidly into thriving towns and ports with wide trading connections across Ireland and further afield. And, significantly, many monastic settlements continued to exist alongside Viking bases, thus complicating the idea that when the Norsemen arrived on the scene, the monasteries were always burned and the monks driven out. This is history underpinned by human impulses, not merely of violence, but of economic necessity, interdependence, and love.

Dublin

This 'human history' is best exemplified in the development of the city of Dublin. Settlements had long existed on a ford across the river Liffey and on the shores of a nearby *dubhlinn* – a black pool – in the river Poddle. In 837, a fleet of sixty Viking ships sailed up the river, and the newcomers established a stockade and base in the area, and put down roots. Doubtless there was violence – and the presence of a defensive wall hints that the Vikings by no means had everything their own way – but the evidence suggests that Christian churches in the district continued to function, implying that the newcomers were as ready to trade as to raid. Indeed, Dublin in time became an *entrepôt* in a vast Norse trading network with tentacles that reached into the Arctic, the Mediterranean, western Europe, and Russia. Walrus tusks and furs, wine, gemstones, and silver were traded through the city; the slave market throve; local jewellery began to show the influence of symmetrical Norse decorative motifs; and Irish traders made use of Viking middlemen to trade their animal hides and timber abroad. This was a new city, and a new world.

Brian Boru

Norse influence in Ireland reached its zenith late in the tenth century – when from the Dalcassian tribe of central Ireland emerged the leader remembered in history as 'Brian Boru', lord of cattle tributes. By 980 Brian controlled all of south-west Ireland, and was putting pressure on *túatha* to the north and east, and on the Norse kingdom of Dublin. In 998 his forces sacked Dublin, and by the early years he had attained a measure of control over the entire island. Only a measure – when rebellion broke out in Dublin, the scene was set for a significant event in Irish history. At Easter 1014, Brian's army gathered outside the walls of Dublin – and into Dublin Bay sailed an international Viking fleet, summoned by the city's rulers. The Norse had the numerical advantage but, when battle was joined at Clontarf, Brian's armies had the victory, though he himself was killed. The Battle of Clontarf is best understood not as marking the end of Viking influence in Ireland, but as altering the balance of domestic politics for good. After all, Brian had attained a form of dominion in Ireland, and other military players now saw that they might achieve the same mastery.

Laudabiliter

The Battle of Clontarf underscores the extent to which
Ireland was connected to wider European economic,
political, and military society. Its elites understood the
power games at play and the importance of outside
interventions, and they were aware of the waxing and
waning of European kingdoms. By the twelfth century,
the Plantagenet, or Angevin, Empire – a loosely-knit
entity stretching from southern Scotland through
England and France to the Pyrenees – was the dominant
power in western Europe. It was governed by Henry II,
who was as hungry for power as his Norse ancestors had
been. Henry was therefore disposed to listen to Dermot
MacMurrough, the deposed king of Leinster, who had
fled Ireland in 1166 specifically to seek the intervention of
the Plantagenets in regaining his lands. And Henry had
another reason to give thought to Ireland: in 1155, Pope
Adrian IV had issued *Laudabiliter*, a decree assenting to
the Plantagenet occupation and governance of Ireland.
The precise contents of *Laudabiliter* have been the
subject of much fraught discussion over the centuries.
Crucially, however, contemporary opinion acknowledged
the Pope's right to dispose of the lands of Christendom
as he chose. Ireland, therefore, was Henry's to take.

Invasion

In the spring of 1169, a small Anglo-Norman military force sailed from west Wales, landed on the coast of County Wexford, and – with the assistance of MacMurrough, who had returned to Ireland to await the intervention he had designed – occupied Wexford town. Late in the summer of the following year, a larger force sailed from Wales and assaulted the city of Waterford on 25 August. The Normans were wholly outnumbered but they held the upper hand just the same, specifically in the form of strategic cunning, excellent armour, and skilled archers, whose arrows were able to rain death upon their foes. This more powerful army was led by Richard de Clare – known in Irish history as Strongbow – and Waterford fell that same day. Much of its population was massacred and, in an indication of his intention to remain in Ireland and develop his lands and a dynasty of his own, Strongbow married MacMurrough's daughter Aoife. Dublin fell a month later, and that momentous year of 1170 ended with Strongbow firmly established in control of a great swathe of south-east Ireland.

Giraldus Cambrensis

Our grasp of the history of this period owes much to the clergyman, scholar, and commentator Giraldus Cambrensis (Gerald of Wales). Giraldus' *Topographia Hibernica* (*Topography of Ireland*, 1187) and *Expugnatio Hibernica* (*Conquest of Ireland*, 1189) are filled with insights into the natural history, culture, and politics of Ireland, and they remain a valuable insight into this distant period in history, despite the fact that he is utterly untrustworthy as a guide. Giraldus might in fact be better described as a skilled propagandist, for he was himself of Anglo-Norman stock, and was a hearty supporter of the Norman intervention in Ireland. To Giraldus, the Irish were barbarous, uncouth, and undeserving of any sovereignty over their own affairs: the long-standing tropes of the Irish as feckless, uncouth, and lazy have their origins in Giraldus' writings. His observations must, therefore, be taken with a very large helping of salt: the doubts that surround the precise wording of *Laudabiliter*, for example, stem directly from Giraldus' claim to have copied out the original faithfully and with honour. And yet he remains a vital source, offering illumination of a period in which such histories are few and far between.

A royal visit

Henry Plantagenet, king of England and Duke of Normandy and Aquitaine, had forbidden Strongbow from sailing to Ireland in the summer of 1170. Though far from displeased at the events unfolding in his name, he was also aware of potential dangers to his position and his throne. His empire was powerful, but his position was far from impregnable. Moreover, Strongbow was himself of royal blood, had disobeyed his overlord's orders, and was now governing his own domain in Ireland – and Ireland, in what would become a persistent thread running through Anglo-Irish affairs, might be used as a springboard, a back door through which England might be invaded. Now Henry moved fast: he demanded his vassal's fealty, and in October 1171 he himself sailed for Ireland. He spent a cold and uncomfortable winter in Dublin and departed in April 1172, never to return, but he was now officially Lord of Ireland, to add to his long list of other titles. His mission to rein in his rivals and tie these new Irish lands to his throne had been accomplished, and the Lordship of Ireland and the Kingdom of England would be bound together for hundreds of years to come.

Dublin Castle

Dublin Castle today is a most agreeable place, composed of museums, green areas, and formal quadrangles, Viking-era excavations, and an array of government offices. The former black pool, or *dubhlinn,* in the river Poddle flows today below the grounds. Dublin Castle has been for over eight hundred years a centre of state power – English, British, and finally Irish – in Ireland, and as such it holds a very particular place in Irish history. The castle was founded on the orders of King Henry's son John, who holds an inglorious position in English history: in the course of his reign, England lost control of most of its French lands. He is also famously remembered as the foe of Robin Hood. But in Ireland, King John is remembered rather differently, for his dealings revealed an astute strategist. He extended the influence of the 'Lordship' north into Ulster and west into Connacht, he introduced a national coinage and the English common law in Ireland, and he ordered the establishment of Dublin Castle, the foundations of which were laid in 1204. The Lordship of Ireland now possessed a great asset: in both symbolic terms and in reality, a powerful focus of authority.

The Lordship of Ireland

By the beginning of the thirteenth century, a delicate equilibrium existed in Ireland. In the north and west, the existing Gaelic order held essentially fast; in the south and east, the English colony – the Lordship – put down roots. Here, new market towns began to develop, and farmland became more intensively worked. Castles were built too, by the dozen. Such building works were a clear demonstration of English authority, but the mere fact of their existence was, of course, also an indication of the essentially tentative nature of the colony. Following the death of King John in 1216, this fine balance began to break down, as waves of legislation – concerning land ownership and ecclesiastical authority – sought to underscore a difference between the English and the Irish. In Rome, Pope Honorius condemned these 'temerarious and wicked' developments, and they led to a sense of economic and cultural shock in Ireland, as the colony expanded and encroachments on Gaelic land increased. Henceforth, control of resources would become a central thread in Irish affairs: as dispossession increased, so there developed a powerful imperative in Irish minds to hold onto what lands were left.

The 'Remonstrance of the Princes'

On paper – on maps and colonial documents – the
Lordship of Ireland appeared secure. Its borders were
expanding, and so was its political and military influence.
On the ground, however, the facts were less certain: the
actions of the colony's leaders were impoverishing the
native Irish, and the resulting tension was creating latent
instability within the Lordship itself. As early as 1318,
the rising disaffection and anger of the native Irish was
encapsulated in a remarkable document written to Pope
John XXII on behalf of Donal O'Neill, Gaelic lord of Tír
Eoghain (Tyrone) in the province of Ulster. This was the
so-called 'Remonstrance of the Princes', the first formal
Irish expression of grievance against English expansionist
policies in Ireland. 'There is no hope whatever of our
having peace with them,' declares the document, detailing
the effects of the 'unbearable yoke' of English 'slavery'.
It goes on to explicitly internationalize the situation,
referring to *Laudabiliter*'s assertion that English policies
in Ireland must be just and fair, and declaring that they
have been anything but. The 'Remonstrance' was a work
of considerable political skill, questioning as it did the
very legal pillars upon which the Lordship rested.

The Bruce Invasion

The 'Remonstrance' was written partly in response to another, frequently forgotten, intervention in Irish affairs. This intervention began in the spring of 1315, when Edward Bruce, brother of King Robert Bruce of Scotland, landed an army on the County Antrim coast. Scottish influence in Ireland had remained strong over the years: Robert Bruce himself was married to an Ulster noblewoman; Scots mercenaries played their part in Ireland's wars; and the leaders of the Lordship contributed men and resources to England's wars with Scotland. In the aftermath of his victory over the English at Bannockburn in 1314, Robert understood that intervention in Ireland at this point was something of a win-win situation: at best, he could install his brother as a client-ruler of Ireland; and at worst, he could create instability in Ireland, and distract English armies otherwise intent on invading Scotland itself. The expedition certainly did bring instability: the military campaign was savage and created chaos, hunger, and misery along the east coast of the country, but the Scottish campaign was a failure. Dublin resisted an assault in 1317, and in October 1318 Edward himself was killed in battle.

Cobhuan De Baus, Rí na hÉreano
Fuair Bás i gCath Fochoaca
14 Deireagh Fómhair 1318
Edward Bruce, King of Ireland,
Killed in Batle of Faughart
14th October 1318

The Statutes of Kilkenny

The Scottish adventure may have failed, but it highlighted fundamental weaknesses in the position of the English colony in Ireland, and these weaknesses only increased with time. The arrival of the Black Death in Ireland in 1348 created a demographic crisis among the colonists, tens of thousands of whom died, though the Gaelic parts of Ireland were much less affected. English power in Ireland shrank, falling back to the seaports. It became increasingly difficult to travel safely from one city to another, and great swathes of farmland fell fallow, for want of labour to work it. In the face of such practical difficulties, the power and influence of the native Irish waxed. Many Anglo-Norman families gradually 'gaelicized', adopting indigenous forms of dress, speaking Irish, and consorting with the Irish as though there was little difference between the cultures. A response to such acculturation came in the form of the Statutes of Kilkenny of 1367, which sought to stem the tide of 'degeneracy' in the Lordship and assert the principle of cultural purity. Use of the Irish language, garb, customs, and sports were banned, to little avail. The Statutes were enshrined in law and were duly ignored.

Reconquest

By the middle of the fifteenth century, the territory controlled by the Lordship of Ireland reached its nadir. For example, the boundaries of the 'Pale' – the land around Dublin more or less controlled by the Crown – shrank back to within a few miles of the city. Soon, however, events were playing out in England that would impact profoundly on Ireland. The Tudor family assumed power in the aftermath of the chaotic Wars of the Roses; henceforth, power was to be centralized ruthlessly. At first, little appeared to change – at the beginning of the sixteenth century, parts of Dublin Castle had to be evacuated, such was the ruinous state of its buildings – but Henry VIII came to the throne in 1509 with the intention of bringing Ireland to heel, and by 1541 he was no longer merely 'Lord' but 'King' of Ireland. The Reformation – the divorce of the English Church from Papal authority, which was spearheaded by Henry later in his career – was embraced enthusiastically by clerical leaders in Dublin, but regarded with horror elsewhere. The further one travelled from Dublin, the more it became apparent that any reconquest of Ireland would be the work of many years.

Surrender and Regrant

Henry had introduced the policy of 'surrender and regrant' as his key initiative in Ireland. Essentially, the policy meant that Gaelic chiefs in Ireland were stripped of their lands, which were then regifted to them, together with formal citizenship and the protection of the law, in return for vows of allegiance and financial tribute to the Crown. Henry's successors, Edward VI and Mary I, continued the Tudor attention to Ireland, and added a policy of limited 'plantation' of the midlands with new, loyal settlers. All three Tudor monarchs were motivated by the desire to pacify and control Ireland without bankrupting the English treasury, but it soon became evident that such notions were overly optimistic. 'Surrender and regrant' did work, but only up to a point: many leading Irish families submitted to the Crown, but many did not. Ireland continued to prove a ruinous drain on the English exchequer, and not even the most fervent Tudor propagandist could assert that Ireland had been secured or pacified. In addition, the religious divisions engendered by the Reformation brought new tensions – and new and unbridgeable divisions between Catholic and Protestant – to the fore.

'Great Terror'

In the course of the long reign of Elizabeth I, a series of events played out that would establish a new Ireland, and a new relationship between Ireland and England. Elizabeth's reign in Ireland is best remembered by the policies in the province of Munster that were carried out in her name. Munster erupted in rebellion in 1569, partly as a result of consistent attempts by the Elizabethan state to break the power of the circle of 'Old English' Catholic families, which dominated the economic life of the region. The Crown responded with a scorched-earth policy, destroying homesteads, crops, and livestock, and executing hundreds of civilians: the Elizabethan adventurer Humphrey Gilbert boasted of the 'great terror' wrought by such actions. A second uprising from 1579–83 created yet more civilian distress, hunger, and wretchedness. Atrocities were committed on both sides; it is estimated that some 30,000 people – a third of the population of the province – died in the course of the second uprising. But Elizabeth had the victory, and now her officials set about a large-scale 'plantation' of Munster, in order to bring the province completely to heel.

Granuaile

Granuaile – anglicized as Grace O'Malley – was the daughter of Eoghan Dubhdara Ó Máille, whose seafaring family was in economic control of a sweep of coast in what is now County Mayo. Under early Tudor policies, the O'Malleys were essentially left to get on with it, but later interventionist English activity began to impinge on the clan's power. Granuaile emerges from history as fearless and independent, a wise strategist and a keen military leader. It was in her interests to limit English influence within the province of Connacht, and she took every opportunity to do so. Granuaile was also highly educated, a fact amply displayed in 1593, when she sailed to England to petition Elizabeth to release members of the O'Malley clan who had been taken captive by English forces. She spoke no English and Elizabeth spoke no Irish, and so, when the two women met at Greenwich Palace, they conversed in Latin. This meeting is one of the more intriguing vignettes of the period, foregrounding as it does a female experience in a history dominated by men. Granuaile remains strongly associated with the Clew Bay area of County Mayo, and with nearby Clare Island.

Trinity College Dublin

The 'College of the Holy and Undivided Trinity of Queen Elizabeth, near Dublin' was founded in 1592. Trinity is by far the country's oldest university, and it represents one of the more enduring traces of the Elizabethan period in Ireland. The college was established with an eye on the collegiate system at Oxford and Cambridge but, unlike those institutions, only one college was ever formed, and Trinity remained the sole constituent college of the University of Dublin. From its inception, the college was a significant locus of Protestant power and authority, and its relationship with Catholic Ireland was strained at best. For the first two hundred years of its history, attendance by Catholics was prohibited. From 1871–1970, the Catholic Church in its turn forbade its flock from studying at Trinity without special dispensation. The new university grew slowly. It was not until the 1700s that it was rebuilt in the form that we see today: a series of elegant quadrangles, surrounded by splendid neoclassical buildings that represent some of the finest eighteenth-century architecture that Ireland can offer. Today, this university 'near Dublin' has been enveloped by the city, and is a dominant presence in central Dublin.

Kinsale

Long-standing concerns that Ireland might be viewed by European rivals as a 'back door' into England were by no means displaced, for in October 1601 a fleet of Spanish ships appeared off the south coast, and anchored off the harbour at Kinsale. The context for this threatened invasion is significant. In the final years of the sixteenth century, the English had made a determined effort to bring Gaelic Ulster into the Elizabethan sphere of influence. The Gaelic leader Hugh O'Neill had been prepared to toe the English line: his family had pledged allegiance to the Crown, and O'Neill himself operated as a mediator between England and Gaelic Ireland. But as land confiscation gathered pace in Ulster, O'Neill suggested to Spain that the road to England did indeed lie through Ireland, and that he could lead a revolt in Ireland as part of the plan. O'Neill was victorious in battle in Ulster; Munster rose again in rebellion, and the English response was ferocious, with a scorched-earth policy creating hunger and death. The Spanish and their Irish allies were defeated at Kinsale on Christmas Eve, 1601 – and now the scene was set for a great cultural and political change in Ireland.

An intrenchment
on here of Quene Sterne by

Camp

The Lord of Thomonds
Towne Campe

The Earle of Thomonds first Camp

The Earle of Thomonds

The Lord Deputes
first Campe

The Flight of the Earls

Hugh O'Neill had been defeated and his lands devastated – but he was not yet vanquished. In negotiations concluded in the aftermath of Elizabeth's death in March 1603, he was permitted to keep his lands and title. He even travelled to London to meet the new Stuart monarch, James I. Soon, however, it became clear what had changed in Ireland, and in Ulster above all: the old Gaelic order had been fractured, and its authority broken as English power took hold now across the entirety of Ireland. This fading of the Gaelic order would, of course, not occur overnight. For generations to come, ancient traditions and ancient language played their part in Irish life, but O'Neill could see the future, and recognize that he would play no role in it. In September 1607, he and his entourage set sail from the harbour at Rathmullan in County Donegal, bound for the European mainland: this sailing was the 'Flight of the Earls', and it marks one of the great rupture points in Irish history. O'Neill died in Rome in 1616, with any dreams of a return to Ireland long since extinguished.

The Wild Geese

The Flight of the Earls would ripple through the history of mainland Europe for generations to come. As time passed, and a degree of Irish influence established itself in Europe, so prominent Irish Catholic families took to sending their sons to the continent, to study and to enlist in the armies of Catholic Europe. This was the beginning of the so-called 'Wild Geese': Irishmen who served governments in France and Italy, Austria and Spain, as well as in such non-Catholic countries as Sweden. The first Irish regiments were formed in the 1590s in the Spanish Netherlands. The Flight of the Earls catalysed the formation of new forces, and an Irish presence in a variety of continental conflicts could be discerned through the seventeenth and eighteenth centuries. At first, English and British administrations in Ireland tolerated discreet efforts at recruitment, feeling that it was better for such young men to fight abroad than, potentially, take up arms in Ireland itself – but from the middle of the eighteenth century, recruitment was banned. From this time the supply of recruits dropped sharply and by the Napoleonic period Irish regiments had been disbanded or folded into existing structures.

The Plantation of Ulster

In the aftermath of the Flight of the Earls, the lands of Ulster's Gaelic leaders were confiscated, and a new state-sponsored endeavour began. This was the Plantation of Ulster, an enterprise vastly larger than any previous attempt at 'plantation' in Leinster and Munster. Its purpose was to settle most of the province of Ulster with large numbers of loyal English and Scottish settlers, with the remnants of Gaelic society banished to the uplands and margins of society. The government had learned a lesson from the settlement of Munster, when too few settlers had been distributed thinly across too much land. In Ulster, settlers were to be concentrated, and segregated from the native Irish, in order to avoid the cross-cultural influence that had hitherto characterized the relationships between newcomers and the indigenous population. In the event, there were relatively few English settlers. Most of this new population came from the overpopulated lowlands of Protestant Scotland, meaning that large parts of Ulster now assumed a distinctly Presbyterian hue. But once more, ideas on paper did not always apply in practice: on the ground, settlers frequently found themselves living cheek by jowl with the indigenous Irish.

The Cuntie of Antrm

Toome

Dunluce   Colrane

Mensourhes

MER VIN T

Wincester Thorn

Maberobey   MAR CHANT   Salsfort of Tough
Thomas
CLOTH   ERN   Phillips

WOR   AYLE
RERS
RS   MONGE   E   R   S

RERS
N   E   R   S
Maberesealt

SALT

HABERDASHERS   ERS

Redford
Thomas

DRAP   E

Phillips   R

S   Dungewen   S

FIS   SKIN   NER
H
MON   Slew Currey

GE
RS

O

R   Moch
S
Good
L
D

GO
S   Movnen
MI
THS

Straban.

The Walls of Derry

Private investment was viewed as being crucial to the success of the Plantation, and the Crown encouraged – and not infrequently cajoled – the guilds of the City of London to contribute to the settlement of the county of Coleraine in northern Ulster. Goldsmiths, tailors, drapers, and other guilds underwrote the plantation of the county, and advertisements exhorted settlers to come west to Ulster, which 'yieldeth store of all necessary for man's sustenance'. In 1610, Coleraine was expanded and renamed Londonderry to reflect this investment, and the old settlement at Derry was refounded as the city of Londonderry, on its hill above the river Foyle. The establishment of this new city was the apotheosis of the Plantation of Ulster. Londonderry was set out as a strict grid of streets behind a circuit of fortifications and capped by a new cathedral, the first explicitly Protestant cathedral to be established in Europe since the Reformation. This was to be a rational place, in implied contrast to the rude and barbarous native Irish who were forbidden from dwelling within the city walls. Local Catholic families instead lived in a marshy area – soon known as the Bogside – outside the walled city.

Scala Pedea

200   100

S Church

The Free schole

The house wherin
ye Bpp: Dwell

Shambles

Queenes Streete

Gracious Streete

N   N   N   N   N

N

N

N

N

N

Ferrey Gate

Gardens

1641

By 1640, some thirty thousand so-called 'planters' had settled in Ulster. There was some mixing of the cultures, but it was no easy matter either for the Gaelic Irish to accustom themselves to this new political and economic dispensation or for the new Scots settlers to feel secure, still outnumbered as they were in this new land. The plantation of Ulster faced its first great test in 1641, as political tensions in England and Scotland sharpened with the approach of the English Civil War. These tensions inevitably transferred to Ireland: in October 1641, Irish Catholic forces sought to take control of Dublin Castle and other strongholds and, while these attempts largely failed, they touched off a wave of violence across Ulster. As the year ended, Protestant settler families were ejected from their homes and lands, upon pain of death, and soon tales spread of atrocities committed by 'Papists' across the province. Both Protestants and Catholics died violently in Ulster in these winter months, as reprisal followed reprisal, but such were the waves of hysteria, misinformation, and propaganda at the time, it is impossible to guess at the numbers of the dead.

Cromwell

The events in Ulster, and the manner in which they were reported and misreported, magnified anti-Catholic sentiment in England and, when the Parliamentary leader Oliver Cromwell came to power following the defeat of the Royalists and the execution of Charles I in January 1649, he had Ireland in his sights. In the context of Anglo-Irish history, few figures polarize opinion as starkly as Cromwell, who has been lauded in England as an early democrat and reviled in Ireland as a propagator of genocide. Cromwell had a profound disdain for Catholic clergy, but he was content to leave individual Catholics to their own devices, so long as they were discreet about their faith. He had, however, a particular hatred of Irish Catholicism, which had been stoked by the horror stories spread concerning the uprising of 1641 and magnified by a specific vein of racial hatred of the Irish that ran through Puritan culture. He also viewed with alarm events unfolding in Ireland, where Royalist and Catholic military factions were closing in on Dublin. And so, on 15 August 1649, Cromwell landed in the city at the head of his New Model Army, the largest Ireland had ever seen.

A 'deluded and seduced people'

From Dublin, Cromwell marched at the head of his New Model Army north along the coast to the port of Drogheda, which was held by a combined Royalist and Irish Catholic garrison. His modern armaments made short work of the medieval city walls: the town fell on 11 September. Over two thousand members of the garrison were executed and, in a deed that would define Cromwell's campaign in Ireland, St Peter's church in the town, inside which a thousand civilians had taken refuge, was burned, killing those inside. English and Irish, Catholic and Royalist alike were among the victims. Many survivors were transported to the sugar plantations of the Caribbean. The events at Drogheda constituted an all-too-evident violation of all the military codes of the day but, undaunted, Cromwell ordered a second massacre at Wexford a month later. The Catholic hierarchy in Ireland strongly condemned Cromwell's actions. He replied to these remarks with a document entitled 'For the undeceiving of deluded and seduced people', which argued vigorously for the moral correctness of the English presence in Ireland. By the time of his departure in May 1650, Cromwell's forces were in control of more than half the country.

The Act of Settlement

By 1652, Ireland was once more under government control. Remaining Catholics and Royalists took to guerrilla warfare, and they became known as 'tories', after the Irish word for a hunted man. Government forces used violence to subdue the countryside: civilians were routinely hanged for crimes actual or suspected, and men hanging from trees became a common sight throughout rural Ireland. It is estimated that by 1660 between one-fifth and one-quarter of the Irish population had been wiped out by war and disease. Now came the Act of Settlement, the intention of which was to eliminate once and for all the power and financial resources of Catholic Ireland. The Act enabled the mass seizure of property and assets, with the result that the percentage of Catholic land decreased from seventy per cent in 1641 to less than ten per cent in 1660. The dispossessed were offered a choice of going 'to Hell, or to Connacht'; that is, death, or stony-soiled reservations west of the river Shannon. As a result of the Act, the 'Ascendancy' was created: a caste of some five thousand Protestant families who would control the lion's share of Irish assets for several hundred years to come.

The Big House

The Age of the Ascendancy in Ireland was epitomized by the creation of walled demesnes across the landscape and, within these lands, the construction of what became known as 'Big Houses'. These were the mansions of newly enriched landed families, and the Big House soon became a dominant feature of Irish life. Some of the Big Houses were big indeed. The great Palladian pile at Castletown in County Kildare and the neoclassical mansion at Castle Coole in County Fermanagh are some of the most striking examples of Ascendancy properties built to impress. Others were smaller and considerably more austere: many a resident of a Big House in Ireland spent a chilly winter in a damp house that simply could not be heated. These houses and estates provided work for local communities. Some also provided elements of welfare at times of scarcity but, as time went on, the Big House and its inmates came increasingly to be associated with concepts of isolation and remoteness. Writers including John Banville (*Birchwood*), Jennifer Johnston (*How Many Miles to Babylon?*) and Molly Keane (*Good Behaviour*) have used the Big House motif to striking effect in their work.

The Siege of Derry

By 1685, a Catholic was on the English throne and events in England and Ireland were again taking a violent turn. The birth of a son to James II and his wife Mary of Modena precipitated the Glorious Revolution of 1688: James was deposed in favour of the Protestant William of Orange and his own daughter Mary II. Sensing an opportunity, Ireland rose in support of James. By December most of the country was in Jacobite hands, and in March 1689 James himself arrived in Ireland. Such opposition to him as remained was largely focused on Protestant Londonderry, which had closed its gates to James's emissaries in December 1688. The Siege of Derry began in earnest in April 1689, when the defenders fired on James as he approached the city walls. Londonderry was in the final throes of hunger and disease by the time the siege was eventually lifted in late July, when Williamite ships broke the boom that had been laid across the river Foyle and sailed up to the quays of the city. It is specifically from the result of the Siege of Derry that Ulster Protestantism derives its motto and maxim of 'No surrender'.

The Battle of the Boyne

In the aftermath of the Siege of Derry, James's position in Ireland worsened: William's strength was enhanced by the arrival of troops from England and William himself arrived in Ireland in June 1690. The scene was now set for a final struggle for supremacy between the two monarchs – and kinsmen – in a battle that took place by the river Boyne in County Meath on 30 June. The Battle of the Boyne was an international event: a combination of French and Irish soldiers fought for James, while William's troops were English, Danish, Huguenot, and German. This dimension underlines the sense in which these Irish confrontations signified the playing-out of a titanic European battle between France on the one hand and an ever-shifting alliance of its enemies on the other. William had the victory at the Boyne – his troops outnumbered the Jacobites, and James himself fled ignominiously to France – and the battle has assumed a considerable significance for unionism. In military terms, it was considerably less significant; in fact, the war in Ireland ground on for another year, until the Jacobite armies were swept away at the Battle of Aughrim in County Galway, on 12 July 1691.

The Penal Laws

The years that followed the Williamite victory witnessed the introduction of a wave of anti-Catholic legislation across Ireland. These 'penal' laws are best understood as a dense maze of statutes that were gradually extended to touch on all aspects of Catholic – and Presbyterian – religious and economic freedoms. Catholic priests were banned and Catholics forbidden from celebrating Mass; Catholics and Presbyterians were banned from voting, or from sitting in the Irish Parliament in Dublin, from carrying arms, purchasing land, and much else besides. Other laws forced the break-up of Catholic-owned lands; and inter-religious marriage was banned, so that Protestant women 'by flattery and other crafty insinuations of popish persons' could not be lured into a union that would cause the transfer of their property into Catholic hands. Such a mass of laws could not conceivably be policed and enforced and, as the eighteenth century wore on, so the impact of such legislation lessened. Yet there is no doubting the force of the Penal Laws: the economic power of Catholic Ireland was shattered in those years, but those laws also had the effect of sealing definitively, in Catholic minds, the relationship between faith and fatherland.

Marsh's Library

In a quiet street tucked behind St Patrick's Cathedral in central Dublin lies a graceful, modestly scaled Queen Anne-style building. This is Marsh's Library, formally inaugurated in 1707 as the country's first public library, and an exemplar of Enlightenment philosophy in Ireland. The eponymous Marsh was Narcissus Marsh, who was successively Provost of Trinity College Dublin, Archbishop of Dublin, and Primate of Armagh. It was during his tenure at Trinity College that he became convinced that the city of Dublin was in urgent need of its own public library, and he was both the prime instigator in creating the Act of Parliament that led to the creation of his library, and the institution's first great benefactor. Marsh's has remained a working library ever since, and is one of the very few eighteenth-century buildings in Dublin still functioning as originally intended. The building is beautifully atmospheric: its old wooden shelves sag under the weight of the leather-bound volumes that fill the library, while its 'cages' – wired-in enclosures into which readers were locked while they consulted particularly valuable books – attest to the fact that library theft was a plague in the eighteenth century just as it is today.

The Royal Hospital

In 1794, the English painter James Malton produced an etching of *The Royal Hospital Kilmainham, North Walk*, showing this handsome building against a Romantic-influenced pastoral backdrop. Dublin's Royal Hospital was already more than a century old at this point, having been completed in 1684, as Ireland was emerging from the long wars of the seventeenth century. The Royal Hospital echoes Les Invalides at Paris in several important respects: architecturally, the building's great courtyard, graceful symmetry, and formal façade resembles its larger and grander French cousin; and functionally, both buildings were designed to house and care for army veterans. It is for this latter reason, indeed, that the Royal Hospital stands as an eloquent exemplar of later seventeenth-century Ireland's new political dispensation. With the country pacified, it became possible to plan and build such a demonstration of military and state power and authority, not in central Dublin, but at rural Kilmainham, beyond the city's western boundaries, and in a place that could not have been readily defended in previous years. The Royal Hospital continued its military function for over 250 years. Today, the restored building, complete with formal gardens and spacious grounds, houses the Irish Museum of Modern Art.

Georgian Dublin

The seventeenth-century 'settlement' of Ireland brought
economic growth, and Ireland's towns and cities were
rebuilt or developed in ways that made manifest the
larger ambitions both of the country's Ascendancy and
of a nascent wealth-creating middle class. Cork, Derry,
Limerick, and other cities witnessed the development of
what today we call 'Georgian' architecture: townhouses
and commercial premises fit for a new, confident
economic and social purpose. This Georgian aesthetic
reached its apotheosis in Dublin, large sections of which
were rebuilt in a form we see today: set-piece squares
characterized by symmetry and a powerful sense of
order, long graceful terraces of townhouses, and a
succession of key civic buildings designed to show off
the city's wealth to the world. The domed Custom House
and Four Courts buildings exemplified this impulse; so
too did City Hall with its rotunda, and the curving walls
of the country's new Parliament House; while the Wide
Streets Commission was charged with sweeping away
much of medieval Dublin's streetscape in favour of
modern boulevards. The Ascendancy enjoyed a splendid
winter season in Dublin: their new townhouses hosted
salons and dinners, and Dublin Castle became the scene
of a succession of glittering society balls.

Swift

The ambivalence of eighteenth-century Ireland's 'betwixt and between' position – neither a part of Britain nor in any way economically or politically autonomous – is encapsulated in the figure of the poet and satirist Jonathan Swift, one of the century's most commanding and influential cultural figures. Swift was born in Dublin in 1667, but spent most of his life travelling between Ireland and England. He had hoped for preferment in his career in the Church, but in 1714 he settled for what was offered to him: an appointment as Dean of St Patrick's Cathedral in Dublin. Thereafter, he became increasingly critical of the governance of Ireland, which he saw worked in the economic interests of Britain. This was epitomized in the Woollen Act of 1699, forbidding the export of Irish wool. In his *Drapier Letters* of 1724 and 1725, Swift urged the Irish to boycott English goods, and *A Modest Proposal* of 1729 captured in scathing terms the economic misery that British protectionist measures created in Ireland. While Swift was a complex character, conflicted in his loyalty to Ireland and to the Crown, he can be understood as a precursor, signalling the Irish nationalism that would develop later in the eighteenth century.

The Irish Parliament

The Irish Parliament was a venerable institution, with roots reaching back to the thirteenth century. It was modelled on the Parliament of England, and was at all times wholly unrepresentative. Its House of Lords was filled from the ranks of the Irish peerage and from the Church – after the Reformation, the Church of Ireland – while the House of Commons was elected on a very limited franchise. The institution was overwhelmingly Protestant, loyal to the Crown, and formally subservient to the Westminster Parliament. Nevertheless, the Georgian period saw the Irish Parliament adopt at times a more assertive position in support of Irish rights and freedoms. This occasional attitude was best expressed in the 1770s, when British military authority was stretched almost to breaking point by the rigours of the American War of Independence. Irish parliamentarians, led by the charismatic lawyer Henry Grattan, now began agitating for the Irish Parliament to assert a measure of autonomy. In 1782, an alarmed Britain granted Ireland legislative independence. This was a victory for Irish patriots, but only a Pyrrhic victory, for the Parliament, in spite of its gleaming new premises, remained the unreformed and archaic body it had always been.

Irish Presbyterianism in America

Irish emigration is often taken to have begun in the nineteenth century, and to consist principally of Irish Catholics leaving for new lives in the New World. In fact, emigration from Ireland began much earlier. By the seventeenth century, Irish communities had been established in Newfoundland and, in the late eighteenth century, Presbyterian emigration from Ireland began in earnest. This movement was a response to the Penal Laws: many among the disenfranchised and politically powerless Presbyterians of Ireland began to seek economic and religious liberty overseas, and between 1717 and 1776, some 250,000 individuals sailed in emigration ships from Belfast and Derry bound for North America. Irish Presbyterian culture left a lasting imprint upon the Canadian province of Ontario, but most of these waves of settlers gravitated towards the British colonies that would become the United States. Following the American Revolution, they embraced eagerly the new nation's principles of religious liberty. The influence of Irish Presbyterianism can be detected strongly in the states of Pennsylvania and Virginia, in the Appalachians, and across the American South, and not least in American politics: Presidents Andrew Jackson, Robert Buchanan, and others were of so-called 'Scotch-Irish' descent.

The United Irishmen

'Grattan's Parliament' had brought a degree of autonomy but the reality was that Ireland was still governed by an unrepresentative minority, and that Catholics and Presbyterians had no political rights. The outbreak of the French Revolution in July 1789 generated new ideas in Ireland, as certain groups began to imagine not Irish autonomy under the Crown, but actual independence, and a formal Irish Republic. These ideas were most enthusiastically embraced in and around Belfast, where Ulster Presbyterianism – already electrified by the events of the American Revolution – was highly receptive to notions of religious freedom, individual conscience, and full democracy. In September 1791, a young Dublin barrister named Wolfe Tone published a pamphlet, *Argument on Behalf of the Catholics of Ulster*, which called for the emancipation of the province's Catholics, but Tone's words struck a chord with the equally politically oppressed Presbyterians of Belfast. The result was the formation of the Society of United Irishmen, the membership of which comprised Presbyterian merchants, manufacturers, and clergymen. The United Irishmen were dedicated to the creation of a secular democratic republic in Ireland – to a new state, one that was wholly separate from Britain.

By 1793, Britain and France were at war, and all trace now vanished of a liberalizing politics on the part of the authorities in Ireland. The United Irishmen were proscribed and the organization went underground. Tone began producing reports for the French authorities, with an eye to encouraging a French invasion of Ireland. In 1795, he travelled to France, where he told the Revolution's leaders of a will in Ireland 'to throw off the yoke of England'. In December 1796, Tone and a French fleet sailed from Brittany and anchored in Bantry Bay, on the County Cork coast. Inclement weather and contrary winds caused the French to beat a retreat, but the Irish authorities, badly shaken by this near-invasion, now bore down ruthlessly on any sign of domestic dissent. Ironically, the ferocity of this crackdown itself generated resistance: in May 1798, a revolt broke out, with most of the fighting taking place in County Wexford. Atrocities were committed on both sides and, by summer's end, some 30,000 people had died. In November, Tone himself was captured on a French ship off County Donegal and transported to Dublin. He committed suicide in his prison cell on 19 November.

The Act of Union

The uprising had been quelled, but the fact that it had taken place at all convinced the British authorities that the ruling class in Ireland could no longer be trusted to keep Ireland in order. The result was a decision to bind Britain and Ireland together irrevocably as one state, one nation. For some years, this policy had been discussed in British political circles. British Prime Minister William Pitt, fearful of what France might yet accomplish in Europe, had long been convinced that only a union of Britain and Ireland, combined with a measure of Catholic emancipation, could bring political clarity and a lasting domestic peace, thus freeing Britain to focus on perilous foreign horizons. The Act of Union was passed in Dublin in January 1800, and the ancient Irish Parliament voted itself out of existence. Now, political power passed decisively to Westminster, with the result that gradually, many Irish political players, with their wealth and patronage, left Dublin for London. The House of Commons saw an influx of one hundred new Irish Members of Parliament, but the opposition of King George III meant that Catholic emancipation, a vital element in this new dispensation, did not materialize.

Maria Edgeworth

In 1800, as the Act of Union loomed, the Anglo-Irish novelist Maria Edgeworth published her first novel. *Castle Rackrent* told the story of a dissipated Ascendancy family on the verge of losing its lands. Its originality and verve ensured its instant success, and helped to propel Edgeworth, at the age of 33, onto the literary stage. A series of other novels followed, together with a vast body of other writings, and Maria Edgeworth became one of the most celebrated writers of the age. Edgeworth's importance and lasting value stem in part from her commitment to realism in her writing, with the result that her work depicted Ireland in all its social, political, and cultural complexity. She lived much of her life on her family estates near Edgeworthstown in County Longford. Her father, Richard Lovell Edgeworth, had a name as a progressive thinker and a fair, liberal, and 'improving' landlord. Edgeworth's reputation declined in the years after her death in 1849, partly on account of the narrative realism that had made her famous. Subsequently, however, she has come to be recognized as a fundamental influencer of the novel form, and one of the great chroniclers of nineteenth-century Ireland.

Wellington

Arthur Wellesley, Duke of Wellington, is one of the most influential figures of nineteenth-century British history. He was a central military leader in the Napoleonic Wars, a significant statesman in the post-war period, and twice Tory Prime Minister. Yet Wellington was not a Briton himself, but an Irishman. He was born in Dublin, of Ascendancy stock, although he was not, perhaps, always pleased to be reminded of the fact. 'Just because you are born in a stable,' he famously and tartly remarked, 'does not make you a horse.' Nevertheless, he stands as the most prominent example of the many Irish figures who carved out significant and highly influential careers in the British political, military, and imperial story. The Wellesley family held estates in County Meath, and the young Arthur was educated in Meath, Dublin, and London, before returning to Ireland to begin his career. At this point, his Irish roots proved crucial. The Wellesley family lacked much by way of money, but they did possess clout, and they used their influence with the Lord Lieutenant of Ireland to obtain for Arthur a commission in the army, thus setting in train a spectacular career that would lead, via Waterloo, to Downing Street.

Moore's Melodies

The early nineteenth century in Britain saw an upsurge of popular interest in Irish music – a cultural change epitomized in the *Irish Melodies*, which were published in ten volumes beginning in 1808. The *Melodies* were the work of the singer, balladeer, and poet Thomas Moore, who was born in 1779 over his father's grocer's shop in Dublin. Following a period at Trinity College, Moore moved to London to train as a lawyer. His destiny then took him to Bermuda and North America, before a return to Britain in 1804. He came back frequently to Ireland: indeed, he held moderately Irish nationalist views, though this did not prevent him living a life at the heart of the British Establishment. He set about writing lyrics to traditional Irish tunes: 'The Last Rose of Summer', 'The Minstrel Boy', and 'Oft in the Stilly Night' are among many of the airs made famous by Moore. His lyrics were designed to appeal to all classes, and yet, many in that same Establishment took a dim view of Moore's works. After all, his Ireland was not merely romantic, it was also grave, stately, heroic, and possessed of an ancient history – and an autonomous identity.

Irish Lights

The stormy Irish coastline has always played a significant role in the country's sense of itself. The ocean renders Ireland as a part of the main and yet separate, the sea lanes understood as less a division than a highway to the great world and the Irish diaspora. And yet the country's seas and coasts have taken many lives and many ships over the centuries. Not surprisingly, then, Ireland's dozens of lighthouses figure largely in the national psyche and, although the island is today divided by a political border, the Commissioners of Irish Lights remains an all-island organization. The history of the Irish Lights goes back a thousand years, to when monks on the long peninsula of Hook Head in County Wexford lit beacons above the Atlantic as a warning to shipping along this treacherous stretch of coast. Early in the thirteenth century, the beacon was replaced by a lighthouse, Ireland's first such, and today this striped sentinel remains among the most characterful and loved of Irish Lights. Others include the 'upside-down' lighthouse on Rathlin Island, where the lamp shines red from its base, and the remote Fastnet lighthouse, on its rock thirteen kilometres south of the County Cork coast.

Emancipation

The question of emancipation – the granting of civil and political rights to Catholics and other faiths in Ireland and Britain – became more pressing as the years passed. Reform was effectively halted by the bitter opposition first of George III and then of George IV, but it was clear to all observers that change must inevitably come. In the end, it was events in Ireland that brought about reform across the new United Kingdom. Reform was spearheaded by an educated, colourful, and cosmopolitan Catholic lawyer named Daniel O'Connell. A talented orator, communicator, and organizer, O'Connell – the 'Liberator' in Irish history – took aim at emancipation as a means of achieving his ultimate goal of the repeal of the Act of Union. In 1823, he established the Catholic Association, a mass movement intended to pressure the authorities to back reform. Elements in the Catholic Church backed O'Connell and, when in 1828 he won a parliamentary by-election in County Clare, the government understood that the game was up. Wellington, who was Prime Minister, brought to the table his understanding of the Irish scene, and, in 1829, a limited Catholic Emancipation bill was approved by Parliament and signed into law by a reluctant George IV.

Repeal

O'Connell and Repeal

O'Connell was now able to focus on his ultimate political goals. In 1830, his *Letter to the People of Ireland* sought to energize the popular will by proposing sweeping political reform, and repeal of the Act of Union. The authorities responded by enacting their own limited reforms to neutralize unrest in Ireland. For example, moneyed Catholics would now be permitted to stand for local government election; and, in 1840, O'Connell became the first Catholic Lord Mayor of Dublin. But O'Connell retained the upper hand: he used the festering grievance of land reform in Ireland to rally the people and, in 1843, he began assembling tens of thousands of people at 'Monster Meetings' to increase pressure on the authorities. The last of these meetings, to be held at the historically resonant location of Clontarf, was banned by the government and, fearing a surge of violence, O'Connell cancelled the event. He was arrested and imprisoned and, when he was eventually released, it became clear that the energy he had previously harnessed in favour of repeal had dissipated. O'Connell died en route to Rome in 1847, by which time a horrifying calamity was unfolding in the Irish countryside.

The Great Hunger

In the summer of 1845, news spread that the potato harvest had failed: the potatoes were emerging from the ground putrid and inedible. The potato plants had been infected with a fungal blight, which was spreading across Europe. Ireland had become dangerously dependent on the potato to feed its swelling population, with the result that the repeated failure of this harvest in the years 1845–9 became a social and human disaster of unparalleled proportions. In 1845, the population of Ireland was nearing nine million. In the Famine years, a million people died of hunger and disease and more than a million emigrated. The population of the island continued to drop for more than a century and the numbers speaking the Irish language went into a sharp decline. The Famine – *an Gorta Mór*, or the Great Hunger – resulted in an unprecedented fraying of social bonds, with families abandoned, and hitherto unimaginable crimes committed to stay alive. As in any social breakdown, the aged, women, and children were disproportionately affected. The Famine has left a profound legacy: scholars speak of a Great Silence, based on shame and trauma, which settled on Irish society in subsequent years.

The Famine and the Future

The role of the British government in the events of the Famine years has been much debated. In spite of claims made by some historians over the decades, there is no evidence that British policies set out to create famine – or genocide, its terrifying sibling – and yet it is undeniably the case that maladministration, dogma, and carelessness fostered and accentuated famine conditions. Laissez-faire economic policies meant that large-scale State intervention never materialized. The government's claims that property taxes levied in Ireland alone should be sufficient to cover the cost of relief works, meanwhile, were palpably erroneous: Ireland was simply not wealthy enough to sustain such costs independently. Such political neglect and carelessness also undermined the politically vital claims made at the time of the Act of Union, that Britain and Ireland now constituted a fused society, with all the collective social and moral responsibilities that this implied. Famine conditions had been experienced repeatedly in Ireland. The severe hunger of 1740–41 had in proportional terms killed as many people as the Great Famine, but the experience of 1845–9 was unique, in that it combined with issues of politics and national identity, to potent and long-lasting effect.

The Irish Diaspora

Not least among such waves of consequences was the creation of an Irish diaspora around the Anglophone world. The United States and Australia, and to a lesser extent New Zealand, Canada, and other countries, played host to swelling Irish communities, composed of individuals and families who had fled the horror of famine, and who were now determined to put down roots in these new lands. There were immediate economic repercussions to this diasporic growth, in the form of a flow of remittances, which helped to sustain many a family in Ireland. Longer-term cultural and political consequences can be perceived in the form of new ideas and influences transmitted into Ireland from abroad. Henceforth, Irish nationalism would instinctively look to the diaspora for financial, intellectual, and moral support. In the United States in particular, Irish Catholic communities and voters came to wield considerable political clout in a form that can still be discerned today. The issue of Ireland now became 'internationalized' in ways that had simply not existed previously, with the result that all parties with a stake in the country were now obliged to consider carefully the global impact of their policies.

The Fenians

The Fenian movement was both a response to the
trauma of the Famine and a demonstration of how
Irish affairs now possessed an international dimension.
The movement developed concurrently in Ireland and
the United States. In the former, the Irish Republican
Brotherhood operated as a secret society dedicated to
resisting British rule in Ireland; in the latter, the Fenian
Brotherhood – named for the Fianna warriors of Irish
mythology – operated openly and freely. By the early
1860s, there were as many as 60,000 Fenians in Ireland.
A rebellion in 1867 ended in failure, but the movement's
leader James Stephens had tapped into the American
diaspora for funds and arms, and demonstrated
what might be achieved in this new international
order. British decisions did not help: three Fenian
operatives were executed for the killing of a Manchester
police officer in November 1867, and this case of the
'Manchester Martyrs' and their dubious trial generated
much public sympathy both in Ireland and abroad for
the Fenian cause. In North America, meanwhile, the
Fenians undertook repeated military operations over
twenty years along the US–Canada border, and this
series of skirmishes caused added irritation in the
already tense relationship between the two countries.

The Church Ascendant

By the middle of the nineteenth century, the Catholic Church in Ireland had thrown off the last vestiges of the relative powerlessness that had accompanied the Penal Laws, to become a dominant political and cultural force in the land. The hierarchy of the Church had been swift to throw its weight behind O'Connell, recognizing that his campaigns would lead to even more Church influence; it was equally quick to denounce the Fenians as a potentially revolutionary force in Ireland. Each interjection was attended to, with all observers of the Irish scene understanding the Church's immensely powerful sway over hearts and minds. The period saw a great flowering of ecclesiastical architecture, best exemplified, perhaps, by the Edward Welby Pugin-designed Cobh Cathedral, the spire of which today soars above Cork Harbour. Maynooth and other Catholic seminaries sent generations of priests to minister in Ireland and abroad. While the establishment of a system of 'national' or primary schools had initially been based on a multidenominational model of education, the system as it in fact evolved, saw most of the primary schools in Ireland controlled by the Catholic Church – a state of affairs which endures to this day.

The 'Irish Question'

From the 1870s onwards, the large contingent of Irish MPs at Westminster played an increasingly visible role in the House of Commons. Charles Stewart Parnell, a Protestant landowner from County Wicklow, was elected to the Commons for the Home Rule Party in 1875, and for the next fifteen years he was pivotal in directing British political life. Charismatic and a powerful orator, Parnell convinced an initially reluctant British Liberal Party leader William Gladstone that Home Rule for Ireland was both attainable and in the interests both of Ireland and Britain. The result was a period in politics in which the 'Irish Question' was dominant: nationalist politicians in Ireland and the Gladstone faction in the Liberal Party championed the cause of autonomy, while anti-Home Rule Liberals, plus Conservative politicians and Ulster unionists, fought bitterly to prevent such a measure being passed. The Liberal Party split as a consequence and, while the prospect of Home Rule tantalized, it was never achieved. Parnell's career was ended by personal scandal, and he died in 1891. The following year, Gladstone brought his last Home Rule bill to the Commons: it was thrown out, and he retired from public life in 1894.

The Revival

The question of Home Rule played out against an altering cultural context. The growth of a Catholic middle class and the supremacy of the Catholic Church in Irish life combined with other factors to foster a rising sense of nationalism and national awareness in Ireland. The pressure for Home Rule was one element in this changing climate; so too was an agitation in favour of land reform that would at length provide small farmers with greater security of tenure. In broader cultural terms, this period saw the establishment in Dublin of a National Library and National Gallery; and of the Gaelic League, founded with the aim of protecting and developing use of the Irish language. The Royal Dublin Society and Royal Irish Academy worked at amassing scholarship, and collecting items both from abroad and from Ireland's ancient past. The latter included priceless treasures such as the Ardagh Chalice and Tara Brooch, dug from fields and bogs where they had lain forgotten for centuries. Such objects possessed tremendous cultural potency, and these rapidly developing collections were combined to form the core of a new Dublin Museum of Science and Art, which evolved into the National Museum of Ireland.

The Gaelic Athletic Association

In 1884, a small group of men met in a hotel at Thurles, County Tipperary, with the intention of formulating a plan to preserve and protect what were considered Ireland's indigenous sporting traditions. The impetus for this meeting and these conversations reputedly came from a stroll one of their number, a County Clare schoolteacher named Michael Cusack, had taken in Dublin's Phoenix Park. As he walked, Cusack noticed little by way of the sporting activity one might expect to observe in a city park on a weekend afternoon. In addition, Cusack and others were mindful of the substantial inroads into Irish life made by such 'British' sports as cricket and soccer. The result of this Tipperary conclave was the establishment of the Gaelic Athletic Association (GAA), which would evolve into one of the most influential forces in Irish life. The GAA's quest was to encourage interest in such historically Irish sports as hurling, camogie, handball, and Gaelic football, and in indigenous Irish culture in general. Elements in the Catholic Church backed the GAA strongly. Archbishop Thomas Croke of Cashel became the organization's patron and, in 1913, Dublin's principal GAA ground was named Croke Park in his honour.

The Abbey Theatre

The Abbey Theatre is Ireland's national theatre. The institution dates its origins to 1899, when – against this climate of cultural 'revival' – the Irish Literary Theatre was established in Dublin by the poet W. B. Yeats, the Ascendancy landowner and folklorist Augusta Gregory, and the playwright Edward Martyn. From its inception, the theatre played its part in the ongoing debate over Irish identity and the meaning of nationalism. For example, a 1902 production of *Cathleen ni Houlihan*, by Gregory and Yeats, portrayed Ireland as the eponymous Cathleen, exhorting a blood sacrifice from her sons. In 1904, the financial support of English theatre patron Annie Horniman enabled the Irish Literary Theatre to become the Abbey, with its own premises in central Dublin. The Abbey is perhaps best known for the public disturbances generated by its productions of John Millington Synge's *The Playboy of the Western World* (in 1907) and Seán O'Casey's *The Plough and the Stars* (in 1926). It is also notable for being the first theatre in the English-speaking world to receive a state subsidy (from 1925). More recently, the Abbey has premiered works by a series of notable Irish playwrights, including Marina Carr, Brian Friel, and Tom Murphy.

SH NATIONAL THEATRE SOCIETY

PREADING THE NEWS
By LADY GREGORY.

N BAILE'S STRAND
and
KATHLEEN
NI HOULIHAN
By W. B. YEATS.

N THE SHADOW
OF THE GLEN
By J. M. SYNGE.

ABBEY THEATRE
UESDAY, DEC. 27, 'O
TO
TUESDAY, JAN. 3, '05.

alls, 3s. Reserved and Numbered. Balcony, 2s. Reserved and Numbered. Pit, 1s

Yeats and Joyce

Many significant cultural figures emerged from this period of extraordinary ferment in Ireland, with the novelist James Joyce and the poet William Butler Yeats among the most prominent. Joyce was born in Dublin in 1882 into a middle-class Catholic family; Yeats was born in Dublin in 1865 into a family with an Ascendancy background and useful social connections. Their two Irish worlds, in other words, were sharply distinct from one another – and it is for this reason that these two figures encapsulate some of the variety that characterized Ireland in those heady days of 'revival'. Yeats identified closely with Ireland's deep past of myth and legend, and with the landscapes of County Sligo in particular. He was a key figure in the nationalist debates of the day: in 1922, he became a senator in the newly established Irish Free State, and in 1923 he was awarded the Nobel Prize for Literature. Joyce departed Ireland in 1904 for exile in Europe: his short-story collection *Dubliners* (1914) illustrates his testy relationship with Ireland, nationalism, and Catholicism, and his later works moved decisively towards experimental forms of modernism. Joyce's fictional universe, however, remained focused entirely on Dublin and Ireland.

Industrial Ulster

The northern province of Ulster had begun to industrialize in the eighteenth century, as the linen industry developed across the region. The mills in the lowlands surrounding Belfast in the east and in the Foyle river valley in the west provided employment, wealth, and a healthy export trade. By the late nineteenth century, shipbuilding and heavy engineering had also become established in Belfast, with the city now intrinsically linked into a wider imperial trade network. The industrialization of the region was in sharp contrast to other parts of Ireland, where an agrarian economy continued to dominate; and this, together with the long-standing Protestant influence across eastern Ulster, ensured that the grain of life and society in parts of the province evolved in notably distinctive ways. In the 1880s, with pressure for Home Rule intense, the Protestant population of Ulster had rallied in support of the Union and against the notion of an autonomous or independent Ireland. Now, with a new century, a new nationalism debate in Ireland, new calls for Home Rule, and new parliamentary arithmetic at Westminster, Ulster's unionist leaders were mindful of a resurgent challenge to their position.

Titanic

The ocean liner RMS *Titanic* was built at the Harland and Wolff shipyards in Belfast, for the White Star shipping line. She was designed with speed, luxury, and modern technology in mind, for such features would add to her allure on the profitable Southampton–New York run. *Titanic* was almost one thousand feet in length; Harland and Wolff was obliged to redesign its yards to accommodate such a vast vessel. Following her completion and successful trials on the Irish Sea, *Titanic* departed Belfast for Southampton on 2 April 1912, with her very existence perceived as a potent expression of Ulster's industrial prowess. She departed Southampton on her maiden voyage on 10 April, called at Cherbourg in France and Queenstown (now Cobh) in Ireland, and was due in New York on 17 April. Near midnight on 14 April, *Titanic* struck an iceberg on the Grand Banks of Newfoundland; just over two hours later, in the early hours of 15 April, she sank, with the loss of some 1,500 lives. The vessel had been designed to stay afloat if four of the compartments in her lower hull were flooded, but the iceberg strike flooded five compartments, thus dooming the ship.

The Ulster Covenant

In the spring of 1912, a new Home Rule was formally tabled at Westminster by the Liberal government of Herbert Asquith, which was maintained in power by the votes of the nationalist Irish Parliamentary Party. There was every chance that the measure would now pass and, in Ulster, unionists mustered in opposition. In September 1912, Edward Carson, the Dublin-born leader of Irish unionism, demonstrated the potential power of his cause by convening a meeting at Belfast City Hall. Here, he signed the Ulster Covenant, a declaration that bound all signatories to use 'all means which may be found necessary to defeat the present conspiracy' of Home Rule. Some 250,000 Ulstermen followed Carson; a similar number of women signed a less martial 'Ulster Declaration'. In January 1913, the Ulster Volunteer Force (UVF) militia was formed. It soon claimed a membership of almost 100,000 and, in April 1914, the UVF received significant arms shipments from Germany. With the Irish Volunteers nationalist militia formed in response, it seemed that the drive for Home Rule would lead to bloodshed in Ireland. But in June 1914, an assassination at Sarajevo set Europe ablaze, and altered the course of events in Ireland too.

A World at War

The outbreak of the Great War in August 1914 paused
the movement towards Home Rule in Ireland. The Irish
Parliamentary Party leader John Redmond exhorted his
followers in the Irish Volunteers to enlist in support of
the war effort against Germany and its allies, and it is
estimated that 250,000 Irishmen joined up to fight. Such
a decision to enlist stemmed, for some, from a sense of
duty and conviction; for others, it was made with more
material calculations in mind, for a spell in the army
meant money for a family at home. Irish soldiers on the
Western Front and elsewhere partook in all the horrors
of that conflict: hellish conditions in the trenches, bloody
experiences in the field, and an estimated Irish death
toll of some 50,000 men over four years of war. For
Ulster soldiers, the experience of war is encapsulated
in the 1916 Battle of the Somme, in which some 2,000
Ulstermen died, along with many other Irish soldiers.
The sacrifice of many lives in the course of the Great War
is remembered in the form of memorial sites in France
and Belgium, and of the Lutyens-designed National War
Memorial Gardens in Dublin.

The Easter Rising

Not everyone heeded Redmond's call to join the war effort. Some 10,000 Irish Volunteers declined to serve the Crown, and the militia became influenced by figures including the barrister, teacher, and poet Patrick Pearse, who was convinced of the need for an armed rebellion against British rule, and convinced too that the Great War provided an opportunity for such a rebellion to be planned and executed. By early 1916, the strategies of the Volunteers had meshed with those other militias including the Irish Citizen Army, headed by the socialist James Connolly, and the female Cumann na mBan group. An armed uprising was their objective, and it began on Easter Monday, 24 April 1916, when the rebels seized the General Post Office and other buildings in central Dublin. The British response was swift and relentless: by the end of that week, large areas of the central city were in ruins, and some 450 people, most of them civilians, were dead. In May, the rebel leaders, including Pearse and Connolly, were executed at Kilmainham Gaol. This proved to be a fatal miscalculation on the part of the British, for public sympathies now swung decisively in favour of the rebel cause.

Collins and de Valera

With the executions at Kilmainham, new leaders came to the fore of Irish nationalism. County Cork-born Michael Collins had been present in the GPO during Easter Week. His relatively junior position ensured that he was not executed, but rather interned in Britain, along with some 3,500 other Volunteers, male and female, in the aftermath of the Rising. New York-born Éamon de Valera had commanded a rebel group in south Dublin. His sentence of death was commuted to penal servitude for life – a decision made, it is assumed, to avoid offending the United States government. As Ireland swung increasingly behind the cause of independence – a movement encapsulated in the United Kingdom general election of December 1918, in which the Sinn Féin nationalist umbrella movement scored a decisive victory in Ireland – these two men became instrumental in furthering the agenda of independence. Collins focused on military and political strategy in Ireland itself; de Valera went to the United States, where he engaged in raising funds and awareness of the Irish nationalist cause. They were colleagues, then, but also rivals, and the complexity of their personalities has ensured that both men remain enduring objects of fascination.

The War of Independence

The incoming Sinn Féin Members of Parliament boycotted the House of Commons. On 21 January 1919, some of them (others were in jail or on the run) met instead at the Mansion House in Dublin, convening what became known as the First Dáil: the first parliament of an Irish state-in-the-making. On the same day, two Royal Irish Constabulary (RIC) officers were killed at Soloheadbeg in County Tipperary, in an ambush that came to be seen as the first act of the Irish War of Independence. The Irish Volunteers gradually came to be known as the Irish Republican Army (IRA), and the conflict between IRA personnel and the British security forces became gradually and inexorably more violent, with civilians all too frequently caught in the crossfire. In September 1919, the British government suppressed the Dáil and, in early 1920, the authorities began recruiting for a new state-supported police unit in Ireland, to operate in tandem with the security forces. The 'Black and Tans' – named for their uniform – came to be feared and hated by civilians in Ireland: they, and a second unit known as the 'Auxiliaries', were notoriously violent and undisciplined, and responsible for many civilian deaths.

The first 'Bloody Sunday'

On Sunday, 20 November 1920, a number of IRA operatives fanned out across central Dublin. They were searching for British intelligence agents working in the city and, by late morning, fourteen agents had been assassinated. Later that same day, a crowd gathered at Croke Park, Dublin's main GAA stadium, located on the northern edge of the city centre, to watch a Dublin v Tipperary Gaelic football match. A group of Black and Tans arrived at the stadium as the match was under way. They fired into the crowd, shooting dead twelve civilians, and two more were crushed to death in the ensuing panic. The incident became known as 'Bloody Sunday' – the first, though not the last, incident in Irish history to bear this title. The result of the day's bloodletting was to touch off a fresh wave of violence: a week later, eighteen Auxiliaries were killed in an ambush in County Cork; and a fortnight after that, much of central Cork was burned in an Auxiliary attack on the city's commercial life. But with both sides bloodied and brutalized, there was a growing realization that this conflict would ultimately have to be resolved with words, and not with arms.

The Treaty

In July 1921, a temporary truce was agreed in Ireland
and discussions began on how a peace treaty might
be formalized. The result was the Anglo-Irish Treaty of
December 1921, agreed by an Irish negotiating team
led by Michael Collins, and a British team including
Prime Minister David Lloyd George and his Colonial
Secretary Winston Churchill. The Treaty stipulated
the establishment of an Irish Free State, consisting of
twenty-six of Ireland's thirty-two counties; the remaining
six would constitute a new autonomous entity within
the United Kingdom. The Free State would remain
within the British Empire, and parliamentarians would
be required to swear an oath of allegiance to the British
monarch, as head of state. The Treaty split opinion in
Ireland. A minority of Dáil members rejected the Treaty:
led by de Valera, they walked out of the chamber. Public
opinion was divided too: a war-weary majority accepted
its terms, but families and communities were split, and
so was the IRA. The British departed from Dublin Castle
after more than seven hundred years, and formally
handed over sovereignty to a new Irish state, but the
scene was set for the brief and bitter Irish Civil War.

tions from the date hereof.

18.   This instrument shall be submitted forthwith by His Majesty's Government for the approval of Parliament and by the Irish signatories to a meeting summoned for the purpose of the members elected to sit in the House of Commons of Southern Ireland, and if approved shall be ratified by the necessary legislation.

[Document bears numerous signatures, largely illegible, including:]

ber 1921

On behalf of the
Irish Delegation.

D. Lloyd George

Austen Chamberlain

Birkenhead.

Winston S. Churchill

L. Worthington-Evans

Hamar Greenwood

Gordon Hewart

On behalf of the Irish
Delegation

Art Ó Gríobhtha

Mícheál Ó Coileáin

Riobárd Barton

E. S. Ó Dúgáin

Seoirse Gabhán Uí Dhubhthaigh

Constance Markievicz

The figure of Constance Markievicz is prominent in the story of these years, as an aristocrat and a central female figure in nationalist politics. She was born Constance Gore-Booth, a member of an Ascendancy family with extensive lands at Lissadell, near Sligo: Constance and her sister Eva were close friends of W. B. Yeats, whose poem 'In Memory of Eva Gore-Booth and Con Markievicz' memorializes the two women:

> The light of evening, Lissadell,
> Great windows open to the south,
> Two girls in silk kimonos, both
> Beautiful, one a gazelle.

In 1900, Constance married Casimir Markievicz, a Polish painter and playwright, but her strong social conscience soon brought her into the mainstream of Irish nationalist life. She joined Connolly's Irish Citizen Army, and played an active role in the Easter Rising, during which it is claimed she killed a policeman, though she escaped the death sentence imposed on fellow leaders of the Rising. In the 1918 general election, she became the first woman to be elected to the House of Commons, though she refused to take her seat, instead becoming Minister for Labour in the First Dáil; and in the aftermath of the Treaty negotiations, she joined de Valera's Anti-Treaty faction.

Civil War

In the early months of 1922, both Collins and de Valera strove to control their respective factions, and to prepare as best they could for a civil conflict that seemed ever more likely. In April 1922, anti-Treaty IRA personnel occupied the historic Four Courts building in central Dublin and, in June, the pro-Treaty government began shelling the complex, in the process destroying a millennium's worth of public records stored there. The operation secured state control of Dublin and, by summer's end, the country's main cities were firmly under government control. Using newly acquired emergency powers, the government ordered the execution of over seventy anti-Treaty operatives, thus magnifying the bitterness sparked by this civil strife. In August 1922, Michael Collins was assassinated in his native County Cork at the age of 31. By early 1923, government control was complete, and de Valera and his followers withdrew for the time being to the sidelines of political life. The Irish Civil War claimed perhaps a thousand lives, and is remembered for its poisonous legacy of social and family division. As civil society was slowly reconstructed following years of violence, the events of the conflict were seldom publicly discussed.

The Irish Border

The Treaty recognized existing facts on the ground, for the Government of Ireland Act of 1920 had already established the detail of a partitioned Ireland. The Irish border now came into existence: a new international frontier line which ran some three hundred winding miles through the country, separating the six north-eastern Irish counties of Derry, Tyrone, Fermanagh, Armagh, Down, and Antrim from the remainder of the island. Although the names of 'Northern Ireland' and 'Ulster' are sometimes used synonymously, three of the nine Ulster counties (Cavan, Monaghan, and Donegal) were in fact excluded from Northern Ireland. This decision was made with an eye on demography: that is, to guarantee a perpetual Protestant-unionist majority population within Northern Ireland. The border had little cultural and economic coherence: it cut through parishes, villages, communities, and property, severed economic hinterlands, and resulted in a good deal of local economic dislocation. Despite this, however, the border rapidly became an established geopolitical fact, and a fixture on the Irish scene.

In Northern Ireland

James Craig was the first Prime Minister of Northern Ireland and, in 1934, he noted that 'we are a Protestant Parliament and a Protestant State'. Craig's observation has been much quoted and misquoted over the years but his words were essentially true. The new autonomous entity of Northern Ireland had been born amid bloodshed, riots, and death. Sectarian violence had been particularly ferocious in Belfast, where the city's Catholic population faced waves of house-burnings and expulsions. It is estimated that some six hundred civilians were killed in the region in the years 1920–22. A process of state-building then began in the infant Northern Ireland, but its fundamentally sectarian nature was at all times visible. Local government was gerrymandered – most notoriously in the predominantly Catholic and nationalist city of Derry, which was nevertheless governed by a unionist council – and Catholics and nationalists were routinely discriminated against in the areas of housing and employment. Meanwhile, as Belfast's industrial sector declined and the early dreams of Northern Ireland as an economic powerhouse dissolved, the region became ever more financially dependent on Westminster.

In the Free State

The new Irish Free State began its existence as a poor and largely agrarian society. The population of rural Ireland was – as had been the case since the Famine – dwindling year by year, while urban Ireland suffered from high levels of unemployment and social deprivation. The slums of Dublin were among the worst in Europe. The new state had been born of revolution and radical politics, but the new governing class soon revealed its profoundly conservative nature, and the Catholic Church now asserted an extraordinary hold over Irish society, with its influence apparent in education, health, and politics. And yet this new state was also capable of innovation. Vast hydroelectric works at Ardnacrusha, near Limerick, aimed at harnessing the power of the river Shannon, were completed in 1929; impressively large-scale housing schemes began to address the country's urgent housing crisis; and a new and – remarkably, given recent Irish history – unarmed national police force came into existence. But such developments could not disguise the challenges faced by the new Irish state: in the years after independence, emigration from Ireland rose inexorably, indicating a fundamental economic failure that lay behind the gloss of the new Ireland.

De Valera's Ireland

Éamon de Valera returned to mainstream parliamentary life in 1927, at the head of his new Fianna Fáil political movement. He came to power in 1932 and would remain Ireland's dominant political figure for the next thirty years. De Valera is remembered for policies which further underscored the cultural and economic conservatism and insularity of post-independence Ireland. He was committed to an ideal of self-sufficiency although, in reality, this led to low levels of economic activity and an ever-increasing dependence on emigration as a means of maintaining social stability in Ireland itself. In cultural terms, meanwhile, such policies led to an atmosphere of stultification. As early as the 1920s, legislation had enabled a widespread banning of films and literature, and this appetite for censorship became an increasingly prominent feature of de Valera's Ireland. In the aftermath of independence, women's role in Irish society had become increasingly circumscribed. The 'marriage bar' of 1933, for example, obliged female teachers and civil servants to resign their positions following marriage, and de Valera's new Constitution of 1937 asserted the natural place of women as being in the home, in the interests of the common good.

The Jews of Ireland

'Little Jerusalem' was the name given to the Portobello district of south inner-city Dublin, adjoining the city's Grand Canal. A Jewish presence in Ireland can be traced back a thousand years, but the community increased in the late nineteenth century, as anti-Jewish violence in Russia and eastern Europe created a wave of migration to Britain, and in smaller numbers to Ireland also. Numbers were never large: by the early years of the twentieth century, there were perhaps four thousand Jews living in Ireland, with more than half of these in Dublin. The streets of Portobello sustained synagogues, kosher stores, schools, and Jewish bakeries. The future Israeli President Chaim Herzog spent his childhood in the district. In 1904, properties belonging to the diminutive Jewish community in Limerick came under attack and their businesses were boycotted – this at the instigation of a fundamentalist Catholic priest. Although there were no fatalities, the attacks led to most of Limerick's Jews leaving the city for Britain. Very few European Jews were permitted to enter Ireland during the Second World War and, in the years after the war, the community contracted markedly, with many families emigrating to Britain, Israel, and the United States.

The Treaty Ports

The Anglo-Irish Treaty of 1921 had stipulated that the British Royal Navy retain facilities at three deep-water ports in the new Irish Free State: at Lough Swilly in County Donegal, and Queenstown (Cobh) and Berehaven in County Cork. Although in theory a continued British presence at these 'Treaty Ports' was a source of vexation to Irish nationalism, it was in practice not an especially pressing issue to a new state with a long list of other problems to address. By the 1930s, however, this context had changed: the geopolitical climate had cooled, with Britain and de Valera's Ireland now engaged in a tariff war in which Ireland, its agricultural exports especially badly hit, was coming off much the worse. This long, ruinous quarrel was resolved in 1938: as part of the agreement, Britain agreed to relinquish its control of the Treaty Ports, it being deemed more important to placate the Irish at this time of rising tension with Nazi Germany. It was a triumph for de Valera, but the British surrender of potentially strategic Atlantic facilities caused some consternation. In the Commons, Winston Churchill criticized the decision as a foolish move in a world drifting towards war.

The 'Emergency'

With the outbreak of the Second World War in 1939, the Irish Free State declared its neutrality. The British made several overtures to the Irish authorities during the war, even offering a public declaration in favour of Irish reunification, if the Free State would only open its ports to the Allies. But de Valera rejected all such offers, in the face of mounting criticism from the United States, Churchill, and others. The years of the euphemistically named 'Emergency' passed amid a climate of fuel shortages, rationing, and censorship, as the war crept closer. Bodies of sailors were washed up in their hundreds along the Atlantic seaboard, the victims of torpedoed ships at sea; a sea mine exploded on a County Donegal beach in 1943, killing nineteen civilians; and Dublin was bombed by German planes in 1941, killing thirty. As many as 100,000 Irish citizens left the country during the war to work in the British war economy and serve in the armed forces – a fact that remained officially unacknowledged until decades later. As for Irish 'neutrality' itself: this was a slippery concept, for it was widely if discreetly understood that the Free State was neutral … in favour of the Allies.

Northern Ireland at War

As an integral part of the United Kingdom, Northern Ireland was – unlike the Irish Free State – officially at war with Germany. Large numbers of troops were based in the province for the duration of the war, reaching a peak of some 300,000 in the approach to D-Day. Northern Ireland played a critical role in the Battle of the Atlantic: the port of Derry was the westernmost safe harbour for the Allies in Europe, with the city transformed into a bustling and colourful British and Canadian army and naval base. The attack on Pearl Harbor in 1941 and the consequent entry into the war of the United States brought thousands of Americans to Derry, adding a further note of glamour to city life and providing, in addition, a welcome economic boost. In some ways, indeed, Northern Ireland was protected from the worst effects of the war: conscription was never applied to the province, in spite of requests from the unionist government at Stormont. But this cushioning effect only extended so far: German air raids on Belfast – the so-called Belfast Blitz – devastated parts of the city in 1941, and killed some nine hundred people.

Elizabeth Bowen

In the course of the war, an Irish novelist supplied useful observations on the Irish scene to the British authorities. 'Dublin is undoubtedly flattered to find herself in the role of a pleasure city,' wrote Elizabeth Bowen, describing the influx of Allied service personnel travelling south from Belfast for a weekend's break from war. Bowen was born into an Ascendancy family, with lands in County Cork. She was very much betwixt and between, epitomizing the divided loyalties felt by many of her class in the years following Irish independence. Although born in Ireland and with deep roots in the country, she spent much of her life in Britain. She noted drily that she was most at home in the middle of the Irish Sea. Her great novel *The Heat of the Day* is set in a London pulverized by the Blitz, but she is best remembered, perhaps, for her early novel *The Last September*, which describes in clear-eyed, unsentimental terms the autumn of Ascendancy life in an Ireland consumed by the War of Independence. Bowen's reputation has waxed and waned. Today, however, she is increasingly recognized as one of the great Irish novelists of the twentieth century.

The 'Mother and Child' Scheme

In 1950, the Minister for Health, Noel Browne, announced plans to provide free healthcare for expectant and nursing mothers. This 'Mother and Child Scheme' was one element in an ongoing modest reform of the Irish healthcare system – Browne was also instrumental in bringing under control the scourge of tuberculosis in Irish society – but the Catholic Church watched these attempted reforms narrowly. It took exception to the notion of excessive state 'interference' in the realm of health, particularly women's health, noting that such moves were 'directly and entirely contrary to Catholic social teaching'. Church disquiet was echoed by the Irish Medical Organisation, which feared that any moves to 'socialize' Irish medicine – along the lines of the newly created National Health Service in the United Kingdom – would result in a loss of lucrative private doctors' fees and influence. The Church regarded the Mother and Child Scheme as a bridge too far and came out swiftly in public opposition. The government rapidly gave way and demanded Browne's resignation. This episode demonstrates the power wielded by the Catholic Church, though it also indicated its limits: the essentials of the scheme were quietly passed several years later by a new government.

The Islands of Ireland

The evacuation of the Blasket Islands in 1953 signified
the final extinction of an age-old culture. The Blasket
archipelago is Ireland's westernmost territory, and the
evacuation of its population was regarded at the time
as inevitable, in that the influence of the modern world
had already resulted in a precipitous fall in the islands'
population. But other factors did not help the islands'
cause: in particular, the new Irish state held ambivalent
views towards its remote island communities sprinkled
along the Atlantic seaboard. A disinclination to invest
in modern infrastructure in these remote communities
meant that the island way of life inevitably struggled in
the modern era. Today, renewed national and European
Union investment has resulted in an island renaissance
of sorts: the population of many communities continues
to decline, but reliable ferry connections and modern
communications have made island life more attractive
and less difficult, and tourists are increasingly drawn
to experience the cultures of Irish-speaking islands off
the coasts of Counties Galway, Mayo, Donegal, and
Cork. Far-flung Tory, off the north-west coast of County
Donegal, is known for its tradition of so-called 'primitive'
visual art, while Rathlin – Northern Ireland's only
inhabited island – is a mecca for ornithologists.

Edna O'Brien

In 1960, the young London-based Irish writer Edna O'Brien published her first novel. *The Country Girls* tells the story of two young friends from the west of Ireland who move to the bright lights of Dublin, make the transition from girlhood to adulthood, and discover the pleasures and challenges of life and love. The appearance of *The Country Girls* was greeted with moral hysteria in Ireland. It was promptly banned by the Irish censor, and denounced by the Catholic Church as filth, and copies of the book were burned in the grounds of the church her family attended in County Clare. O'Brien herself, in the years that followed, came to exemplify the changing face of Irish culture. To conservative Ireland, she was a voice telling stories that were best kept silent: of sexual awareness and autonomous identities in what was still a repressive society; of women's experiences, of exile, and of different worlds that were there for the taking. To progressive Ireland, she symbolized the spirit of change and liberation discernible in Ireland in the post-war years. Today, O'Brien's reputation is secure, and she is recognized as an influential and highly original voice in Irish writing.

The Road to the Troubles

By the mid-1960s, the political climate of Northern Ireland
was beginning to alter. The expansion of free education
across the United Kingdom, which had been set in
motion in the 1940s – the so-called 'Butler Acts', named
for the Conservative politician who piloted the measures
through Westminster – had resulted in the appearance
of a new generation of grammar-school- and university-
educated Catholics, who were no longer prepared to
put up with the routine discrimination handed down by
the unionist administration at Stormont. The politics of
these years was profoundly influenced by the civil rights
movement in the United States: Catholics identified
closely with the struggle for equality championed by
such figures as Martin Luther King. The Northern
Ireland government and Ulster loyalist groups reacted
sharply to the onset of Catholic and nationalist civil
rights marches and demonstrations. In early January
1969, a civil rights march from Belfast to Derry was
attacked at Burntollet and broken up by loyalist
demonstrators. The refusal of the police to intervene and
end the disturbance shattered any remaining nationalist
trust in civil authority. By the summer, British troops
were deployed to Northern Ireland for the first time, in
an attempt to keep the peace.

The Troubles

The 'Troubles' afflicted Northern Ireland for over thirty years, and caused the deaths of over 3,000 people, most of whom were civilians. The majority of these deaths took place in Northern Ireland itself, but violence also occurred in Ireland, Britain, and further afield. This was a conflict with roots reaching deep into a complex and tortured past and, at its most stark, involved a bitter confrontation between the forces of the British state and Irish republicanism. The nature of the Troubles, however, was complicated by the presence of other players, including rogue elements within the security services, and a range of Ulster loyalist and Irish republican splinter paramilitary groups. Although civil society and everyday life continued for the duration of the Troubles, it was by no means life 'as normal': indeed, the texture of life in Northern Ireland became profoundly abnormal. Civilians became accustomed to such features as 'peace walls', designed to separate rival neighbourhoods from each other. Shoppers in Belfast had to pass through elaborate security cordons in order to access the city's commercial heart, and the segregation of Protestants and Catholics became an increasingly prominent and absolute feature of life as the years passed.

The Second 'Bloody Sunday'

In the period following Burntollet, the security situation worsened markedly: sectarian tensions became further inflamed, and violence, riots, and general unrest spread across Northern Ireland. The decision by the Stormont government to introduce internment without trial led to further disorder, with many demonstrations held across the province. On Sunday, 30 January 1972, an anti-internment march took place in Derry. It was banned by the authorities, but went ahead regardless and, as the demonstrators gathered below the old city walls of Derry, gunfire was heard. Within minutes, thirteen men had been shot and killed, and a fourteenth died later of his injuries. The official investigation cleared the British army personnel on the ground of any wrongdoing, and claimed that some of the dead men were IRA operatives. In 2010, however, a second investigation – the Saville Inquiry, convened by the British government – exonerated the dead men, and found that the Army's actions on the day were 'unjustified and unjustifiable'. Bloody Sunday was an event of ghastly distinction, in that the victims had been killed publicly by the state, and so Saville is widely regarded as having been a necessary act in staunching the most notorious wound of the Troubles.

In Europe

On 1 January 1973, Ireland and the United Kingdom joined what was then the six-nation European Economic Community (EEC), forerunner of the European Union (EU). Both states had originally applied to join the EEC in 1961: France vetoed the British application, and as a result of the economic connections between the UK and Ireland, the latter withdrew its application. From the outset, the two states held markedly different attitudes towards the European project: while successive British governments displayed a consistent ambivalence towards the idea of an evolving political union, Irish state papers from the 1960s demonstrate a fundamental acceptance of the concept of European integration. Ireland's marked Europhilia can be explained by the experience of colonialism: the EU counterbalances a history of British domination and, in the decades since accession to the EU, Ireland has developed its ties to Europe, and considerable EU funds have been invested in developing Ireland's infrastructure. EU capital has also been invested in Northern Ireland: and, while many unionists reject the notion of a European role in the province, many nationalists seek to underscore Northern Ireland's wider European identity and destiny.

The Presidents of Ireland

The Irish Free State retained the British monarch as head of state, represented by a governor-general – and this situation continued until the new Constitution of 1937 created the office of a directly elected *Uachtarán na hÉireann*, or President of Ireland. To date, there have been nine Presidents. They are elected for an initial term of seven years, and may hold office for a maximum of two terms; their powers are extremely circumscribed. Until relatively recently, the Presidency was a low-profile affair, but this changed decisively in 1990 with the election of the lawyer and human rights advocate Mary Robinson, who sought to refresh the office and bring it closer to the people. Robinson was succeeded by a second high-profile female President: Mary McAleese was also the first holder of the office to come from Northern Ireland. The current President is the poet and former Labour Party politician Michael D. Higgins. These three have succeeded in using the symbolism and human face of the Presidency to good effect, both domestically and on the international stage. The official residence of the Presidents of Ireland is the imposing former Viceregal Lodge – now *Áras an Uachtaráin* – in Dublin's Phoenix Park.

Corncrake

The corncrake – an elusive, seldom-glimpsed, ground-nesting bird – has come to symbolize the shrinking biodiversity of the island of Ireland. The corncrake was once widespread in Ireland: its instantly recognizable call was a common sound in summer meadows and hayfields up and down the land, and a loved feature of Irish folklore and oral culture. However, the mechanization of agriculture destroyed nesting sites, and has caused the corncrake's extinction in virtually all of mainland Ireland. Today, the bird breeds successfully only on a few offshore islands – notably on the north-coast redoubts of Tory and Rathlin, where meadows are managed specifically with the corncrake in mind. The degradation of Ireland's bogs – unglamorous but rich habitats, as well as highly efficient carbon stores – has also been widespread and devastating to wildlife; and these are but two tales among many. There are also, of course, positive stories to report: notably that of the pine marten, which was given official protection in the 1970s, and which has now successfully recolonized most of Ireland. Precious landscapes have also received protection, including the remarkable karst plateau of the Burren in County Clare, with its marvellous growth of orchids, gentians, and other rare flora.

Catholicism and Ireland

The power of the Catholic Church in Irish life seemed unquestioned for a large part of the twentieth century. By the early 1970s, however, there were signs that the position of the institution was weakening: the numbers of young Irish entrants to the religious life began a precipitous decline, and many of Ireland's seminaries began to close for want of numbers. The arrival of Pope John Paul in 1979 – the first papal visit to Ireland – was extensively covered in the media, and the pontiff attracted vast crowds to Dublin and other cities but, in hindsight, it can be observed that this demonstration of faith and allegiance to Rome, though notable, did not halt Ireland's transition to an increasingly secular society. Change was coming. For example, in 1935, it had become illegal to sell contraceptive devices. This situation was increasingly challenged from the early 1970s onwards and, in 1979, the law was altered to permit the purchase of the contraceptive pill by prescription for the purposes of 'bona fide family planning' – that is, for use by married couples. This measure was an 'Irish solution to an Irish problem' but it was also a forerunner of social revolutions still to come.

The 'X Case'

In 1983, voters in the Republic voted to insert the 'Eighth Amendment' into the Irish Constitution, asserting the equal right to life of the pregnant woman and unborn child. The amendment passed by a majority of 66%. The campaign in favour of the amendment had been championed by the Catholic bishops, and the referendum result was viewed as an emphatic victory for traditional Catholic morality in Ireland. Critics warned that the new amendment was vaguely worded, that medical professionals would struggle to interpret it, that the life of the pregnant woman would potentially be put in danger, and that the essential consequence of the amendment would be to continue and enable the 'export' of Ireland's abortions. In 1992, the so-called 'X Case' underscored the difficulties implicit in the Eighth Amendment. A teenage rape victim – 'X' – who had travelled to London for an abortion was compelled by an Irish court injunction to return home; the Supreme Court subsequently upheld her right to a termination. Subsequent referendums guaranteed the right of pregnant women to travel, and to be supplied with information on abortion services, but abortion itself remained illegal in the Republic.

Church scandals

From the 1990s onwards, a succession of scandals undermined the authority of the Catholic Church in Ireland. One of the earliest revealed hypocrisy at the highest levels of the Church hierarchy: in 1992, the Bishop of Galway, Eamonn Casey, was revealed to have fathered a son as part of a relationship with an American. But this titillating episode would soon seem small-scale as a variety of horrors came to light, revealing sexual and physical abuse inflicted on children by priests, nuns, and other members of religious orders across Ireland. The details were appalling: bishops, rather than deal decisively with abusive priests, had instead moved them from parish to parish, thus ensuring that more and more children were abused. Deferential state authorities had declined to take action even when supplied with incontrovertible evidence of crimes. A series of inquiries, including the Ferns Report (2005) and the Ryan Report (2009), sought to provide authoritative accounts of the abuse suffered by generations of children in Church-administered, state-funded institutions, but evidence has continued to emerge slowly, revealing the Church in Ireland as unable – or for financial reasons, unwilling – to definitively confront its crimes.

Incarceration

The history of independent Ireland is marked by deeply disturbing policies favouring incarceration: specifically, the incarceration of children, women, and other social groups deemed to exist outside the economic and social mainstream. By the middle of the twentieth century, rates of incarceration of Irish citizens were among the highest in the world, with a system of institutions across the country – Magdalen laundries, orphanages, and so-called 'industrial schools' – housing thousands of inmates at any given time. The history of the Magdalen laundries is especially shocking. Girls and women were placed in such state-funded institutions, often at the request of their families, for a variety of 'crimes' ranging from excessive flightiness to pregnancy outside wedlock. The children born to pregnant inmates were then processed for adoption, which was often carried out illegally. The 'Magdalens' worked without remuneration and, for the most part, in conditions of strict silence. Women frequently spent the greater part of their lives in such establishments, and were often stripped of their very name, leading to great difficulties later in sourcing their personal records and those of their children. The state issued a formal apology in 2013, but the official compensation scheme has been widely criticized.

The Good Friday Agreement

The Belfast or Good Friday Agreement of 1998 is a binding international treaty designed to end three decades of violence in Northern Ireland. In the years leading up to the signing of the Agreement, discussions had slowly grown in scale and pace: these conversations involved some – though not all – of Northern Ireland's political parties, and the British and Irish governments, with the administration of US President Bill Clinton also playing a significant role. In addition, the IRA had declared a first, and then a second, ceasefire, in the process creating a semblance of normal life and politics on the streets of Northern Ireland itself. The broader context of the talks was also highly significant. There was widespread recognition within Irish republicanism that an armed conflict could not in itself achieve its stated objective of a reunited Ireland; the UK government was eager to see a definitive end to ruinous IRA attacks on economic and commercial targets in Britain itself; and the Irish government was willing to relinquish its long-standing territorial claim on Northern Ireland. Following a tense and exhausting final period of negotiation, the various parties reached an agreement at Belfast at Easter 1998.

Imperfect peace

The Good Friday Agreement established a devolved administration in Northern Ireland, based on principles of power-sharing and 'parity of esteem' between unionist and nationalist communities. Political prisoners were to be released from prison, troop levels reduced, and paramilitary arms put out of commission, and, crucially, it was agreed that the political status of Northern Ireland could only change with the consent of its citizens. The tentative peace was shattered in August 1998, when twenty-nine people were killed by a car bomb planted by dissident republicans at Omagh in County Tyrone, in what was the deadliest single episode of the Troubles. But the peace in Northern Ireland has held, to a greater or lesser extent, in the years since the signing of the Good Friday Agreement, and has withstood several suspensions of devolved government. The shape of the peace accord has been subjected to increasing scrutiny. In particular, its acceptance of the principle of two distinct communities in Northern Ireland is widely judged to be unhelpful to the possible evolution of a shared civic space. Segregation of communities and of education continues to be a fundamental element of life in a society living with peace arrangements both flawed and necessary.

Two Nobels

In the course of the 1990s, two Irish citizens received Nobel Prizes. In December 1998, the nationalist politician John Hume, together with his unionist opposite number David Trimble, received the Nobel Peace Prize at Oslo 'for their efforts to find a peaceful solution to the conflict in Northern Ireland'. Hume is widely regarded as the prime architect of the Good Friday Agreement. He had worked for a peace settlement throughout the Troubles, and as early as the 1980s he was in private discussions with republican representatives, with the aim of charting a path towards a ceasefire, maintaining these talks in the face of considerable vituperative comment. Three years before Hume's award, the poet Seamus Heaney had received the Nobel Prize for Literature in Stockholm 'for works of lyrical beauty and ethical depth, which exalt everyday miracles and the living past'. Hume and Heaney were educated at the same Derry grammar school. They are representative of the generation of Northern Ireland nationalists who benefited from the education reforms of the 1940s, and who were profoundly shaped by the civic politics of the 1960s before embarking on monumental and deeply influential careers.

A Tiger and a Bail-Out

For most of its existence as an independent state, Ireland had been in the economic doldrums, with years of sluggish growth and extremely high levels of emigration. By the late 1980s, however, there were indications that changes in strategic planning were bearing fruit. A comparatively low rate of corporation tax, combined with an English-speaking and well-educated workforce, was attracting large companies to Ireland, and employment levels were beginning to rise. By the 1990s, the Irish economy (though still small by international standards) was expanding rapidly. Soon, the property market had exploded, and the term 'Celtic Tiger' began to circulate, this being a reference to the economies of so-called 'Asian Tiger' nations, which were similarly prospering. Beginning in 2007, the global banking crisis put paid to the country's ostensible economic miracle, and revealed an Irish banking sector that was poorly capitalized and facing imminent bankruptcy. The state bailed out the banks and, by 2010, it was itself forced to seek a bail-out from the European Union. The economic shock of those years was profound and deep-seated, and generated lasting resentment from citizens forced to bear the cost of an economic calamity not of their making.

Two Referendums

The changing social climate of the Republic of Ireland is nowhere better demonstrated, perhaps, than in the results of two referendums, held in 2015 and 2018. Homosexual activity in Ireland – in another indicator of the waning of the power of the Catholic Church – had been decriminalized in 1993 and, as the idea of marriage equality began to be widely accepted in western Europe and elsewhere, so a campaign gathered pace in Ireland to enshrine this right in the Constitution. The proposal was vigorously opposed by conservative and Catholic lobby groups: but, when in May 2015 the public referendum took place, it passed decisively, with 62% of voters approving the proposal. In May 2018, another referendum approved – by 66% – a measure permitting the Irish parliament to legislate for the introduction of abortion in Ireland. This result, which followed an even more fraught and vigorously debated campaign, was generally viewed as reflecting the Catholic Church's perhaps terminal loss of authority in Ireland, and as demonstrating powerfully the altered face of Irish society in the twenty-first century. In Northern Ireland, same-sex marriage remains illegal, while the issue of abortion is governed by harsh laws first passed in the Victorian period.

Brexit and the future

As the two parts of Ireland look into the future, much is unclear. The Brexit referendum of 2016 has contributed substantially to this lack of clarity, though it also has demonstrated very effectively that Ireland's future is as linked as was its past to the currents, ebbs, and flows of the wider world. For the Republic, the future emphatically means a close and enduring relationship with the European Union. For Northern Ireland – the electorate of which voted decisively to remain part of the EU – the future is even more dependent on what may happen elsewhere. In particular, should Scotland opt in due course to leave the United Kingdom, then the effect on the psyche of Northern Ireland unionists will – given the long historical ties between Scotland and Ulster Protestantism – be profound. This in turn connects to the destiny and future shape of the Republic: will it remain a state within its present borders, or is a unified Irish state more likely now than ever? It would be prudent, perhaps, for both entities on the island of Ireland to begin to prepare for a future the shape of which remains, for now, out of sight.

Index

Image credits